THE SHOOTING SCRIPT

THE KIDS ARE ALL RIGHT

THE SHOOTING SCRIPT®

THE KIDS ARE ALL RIGHT

Screenplay by
Lisa Cholodenko & Stuart Blumberg

A Newmarket Shooting Script® Series Book
NEWMARKET PRESS • NEW YORK

Screenplay © 2010 by TKA Alright LLC/UGC PH. All rights reserved.
Motion Picture Artwork, Photography, and Text © 2011 by Focus Features LLC.
All rights reserved. Used by permission.

The Newmarket Shooting Script® Series is a registered trademark of
Newmarket Publishing & Communications Company.

This book is published simultaneously in the United States of America and in Canada.

All rights reserved. This book may not be reproduced, in whole or in part,
in any form, without written permission. Inquiries should be addressed to:
Permissions Department, Newmarket Press, 18 East 48th Street, New York, NY 10017.

FIRST EDITION

10 9 8 7 6 5 4 3 2 1

ISBN: 978-1-55704-937-7

Library of Congress Catalog-in-Publication Data available upon request.

QUANTITY PURCHASES

Companies, professional groups, clubs, and other organizations may qualify for special terms when ordering quantities of this title. For information e-mail sales@newmarketpress.com or write to Special Sales, Newmarket Press, 18 East 48th Street, New York, NY 10017; call (212) 832-3575 ext. 19 or 1-800-669-3903; FAX (212) 832-3629.

Website: www.newmarketpress.com

Manufactured in the United States of America.

OTHER BOOKS IN THE NEWMARKET SHOOTING SCRIPT® SERIES INCLUDE:

About a Boy: The Shooting Script	*The Hurt Locker: The Shooting Script*
Adaptation: The Shooting Script	*Juno: The Shooting Script*
The Age of Innocence: The Shooting Script	*Knocked Up: The Shooting Script*
American Beauty: The Shooting Script	*The Ice Storm: The Shooting Script*
A Beautiful Mind: The Shooting Script	*Little Miss Sunshine: The Shooting Script*
The Birdcage: The Shooting Script	*Michael Clayton: The Shooting Script*
Black Hawk Down: The Shooting Script	*Milk: The Shooting Script*
The Burning Plain: The Shooting Script	*The People vs. Larry Flynt: The Shooting Script*
Capote: The Shooting Script	*Please Give: The Shooting Script*
The Constant Gardener: The Shooting Script	*The Savages: The Shooting Script*
Dan in Real Life: The Shooting Script	*The Shawshank Redemption: The Shooting Script*
Dead Man Walking: The Shooting Script	*Sideways: The Shooting Script*
Eternal Sunshine of the Spotless Mind: The Shooting Script	*Slumdog Millionaire: The Shooting Script*
	The Squid and the Whale: The Shooting Script
(500) Days of Summer: The Shooting Script	*Stranger Than Fiction: The Shooting Script*
Funny People: The Shooting Script	*Synecdoche, New York: The Shooting Script*
Gods and Monsters: The Shooting Script	*Taking Woodstock: The Shooting Script*
Gosford Park: The Shooting Script	*Traffic: The Shooting Script*
Human Nature: The Shooting Script	*The Truman Show: The Shooting Script*

OTHER NEWMARKET PICTORIAL MOVIEBOOKS AND NEWMARKET INSIDER FILM BOOKS INCLUDE:

Angels & Demons: The Illustrated Movie Companion	*Gladiator: The Making of the Ridley Scott Epic Film*
The Art of How to Train Your Dragon	*Good Night, and Good Luck: The Screenplay and History Behind the Landmark Movie**
The Art of Monsters vs. Aliens	
The Art of X2*	*Hotel Rwanda: Bringing the True Story of an African Hero to Film**
The Art of X-Men: The Last Stand	*The Jaws Log*
Bram Stoker's Dracula: The Film and the Legend*	*The Mummy: Tomb of the Dragon Emperor*
Chicago: The Movie and Lyrics*	*Ray: A Tribute to the Movie, the Music, and the Man**
Dances with Wolves: The Illustrated Story of the Epic Film*	*Saving Private Ryan: The Men, The Mission, The Movie*
Dreamgirls	*Schindler's List: Images of the Steven Spielberg Film*
E.T. The Extra-Terrestrial: From Concept to Classic*	*Superbad: The Illustrated Moviebook**
	Tim Burton's Corpse Bride: An Invitation to the Wedding

*Includes Screenplay

CONTENTS

A Conversation with the Screenwriters	vii
The Shooting Script	1
Stills	99
Cast and Crew Credits	107
About the Filmmakers	113

A CONVERSATION WITH THE SCREENWRITERS

Q: *The ampersand in the credits of* **The Kids Are All Right** *would seem to indicate that you wrote this script together. Is that the case?*

Lisa Cholodenko: Stu and I had been acquaintances for years in New York. One day we ran into each other in a coffee shop in Los Angeles (where I'd relocated a year earlier) and he asked me what I was up to. I told him I was writing a new script but I'd just started and was hitting some walls.

Stuart Blumberg: She said, "I'm writing a mainstream movie about a modern gay family." And I said: "That's funny, because I want to write something more indie, like [the movies] you do."

LC: I pitched him the idea for *Kids*—the story of a fairly square lesbian couple, their two teenage children, and the sperm donor who made it all possible. Without missing a beat, Stuart said:

SB: I was a sperm donor in college.

LC: Hearing that, I had a flash epiphany. I thought: "My girlfriend and I are having a kid with a sperm donor and Stuart's been a sperm donor. I'm lonely writing alone and I bet he is too." So I blurted out: "You want to write this script with me?" I guess it was kismet because we started working together the next day.

SB: Which was interesting because until that point neither one of us had collaborated on a script before. We were both solo screenwriters. But I told Lisa that I'd wanted to write something more indie in spirit like she did. And Lisa told me she'd wanted to write something a little more commercial like I did. So we kind of entered into the partnership as this experiment to see if we could blend our two styles and meet in the middle.

Q: Did you just start writing scenes, or go at it another way?

LC: It was a long process; it took us over four years.

SB: We sat side by side for months on end pounding out the outline and first draft. Every single scene, character, and line of dialogue was reworked at least ten times.

LC: We asked each other hard questions about these characters, shaped them, and put them into contrast with each other. It was a long process because we were determined to get all the pieces right—the story, the plot, the character arcs, etc. But mostly we were driven to create multidimensional characters that resonated with us personally. We didn't let up until the characters were dynamic and made sense psychologically. Beyond that we agreed to question (and throw out) anything that felt too earnest or politically correct. All this stuff was a process.

SB: It was an interesting dynamic writing together; men and women are different. Sometimes I'd sit at the computer and say, "Okay, I've only got so much time, so let's get started." But she'd say: "No, no, tell me about your weekend. What happened?" "No, we really have to start." "No, I need to process. I need to ease into this."

LC: It's a journey inventing characters that feel real and are interesting and have issues worth putting on the screen. Once I was lamenting to my girlfriend that I didn't know if the script was any good. And she said: "Just keep writing 'til you break your own heart. If it resonates with you, and you care about these people, then you're on the right track." That idea became a kind of mantra for us. I think we knew that if we weren't feeling it, no one else would.

Q: Wasn't the film set for production years earlier?

LC: Yes, Stuart and I had been writing for about a year and a half, and I was simultaneously trying to get pregnant—which I did. We tried to get production up in 2005-2006, hoping to make the film and get it all done *before* I had the baby, but that didn't exactly time out. By the time the financing was coming together, I was just too pregnant to direct the film. So I had my son and spent the next year and a half learning how to be a mom.

Even then, Stuart and I continued to write revisions and the script got better and better.

Q: You shot the movie on film, right?

LC: [Cinematographer] Igor Jadue-Lillo and I used 35 millimeter [film]. I love film [stock]. I didn't want a dense, hyper-real look [from digital]. I wanted to see some grain in the picture. I wanted subtle play with light and shadow. I like the imperfections you get with celluloid. For me, form and content in film are inseparable. We were presenting a story about a family who finds itself in a bit of an emotional mess. It seemed wrong to offer that up in a pristine package.

Q: Were you intent from the beginning that audiences take away a message from the movie?

LC: Yes. But not in the way one might expect. We wanted the story to be an exploration of what all families face, especially families with children. We wanted to explore the anxiety and comedy and pain and pathos of watching your family shape-shift on you. Whether you're gay or straight or single or interracial or whatever—everybody has a similar trajectory; all families face similar challenges—the emotional rites of passage, the choices made, and the challenge of sticking things out and hanging together as a unit.

SB: If there's any message about gay marriage in the story, it has to do with that joke, "Gay people deserve to be as miserable as straight people." I think when Lisa and I started writing *The Kids Are All Right*, we were saying, "This is something that exists, this is everywhere. Let's start from that position and explore the story that comes out of that." We really focused on human beings, not issues. Hopefully the story is rich and complex enough to compel an audience on its merits.

LC: I'm not really a political person, especially on this topic. I'm impatient with the debate around gay people having the right to marry and raise children. For me, these are basic human rights issues and shouldn't be up for debate in the first place. In any case, I feel I can best serve the "cause" as a creative person.

I know some will say, "Oh, okay, there's an unconventional family, two moms and their kids." But to me, it looks pretty typical. We're putting this family on-screen in a way that isn't part of a politicized environment. It's just, "Here's this family." I guess you could say we're making a statement or being political in a subversive way. We consciously chose to present this world as normal and average.

Stuart and I were clear that we didn't want to make a "cause" film. We wanted to make a comedy-drama and focus on the deeper aspects of family dynamics. We wanted to show these people, warts and all, and not hold them to any higher standard than we would hold straight people or anyone else.

SB: Our story's family is as wonderful and troubled and flawed and impractical as any family. With stories like this, you get to delve into why human beings behave the way they do. And that's ultimately what kept it interesting to us for so long.

Q: *What did Mark Ruffalo bring to the role of Paul?*

LC: Paul is a richer character with Mark playing the role. I've always wanted to work with Mark, ever since seeing him in *You Can Count On Me*. I knew he'd be perfect playing a guy you're drawn to, and even care about, even though he makes lousy choices and hurts people. It's hard to pull off that kind of character and keep him sympathetic. But if anyone could do it, Mark could. He has that ineffable thing that great actors share: the ability to be light and dark simultaneously and keep the audience connected.

Q: *Was Julianne Moore always your first choice?*

SB: Sure, we wrote the character of Jules with Julianne in mind.

LC: Julie and I met about ten years ago and talked about wanting to work together. I sent her an early draft of *The Kids Are All Right* and she attached herself right away. When the movie didn't go in 2005, she stayed attached and committed. Stu and I kept working on the script and sent her drafts along the way. She and I would check in every few months and discuss the revisions—how things had changed for the characters and why. She got to know her character in a very organic way.

Q: *While you were writing for Julianne all along, with no one cast as Nic was there by default a lot of Lisa in Nic?*

LC: There are parts of myself in Nic, strains of my personality, but I wasn't a stand-in for that character. Nic is a conflation of people Stuart and I know, with aspects of ourselves sprinkled in.

In terms of casting Nic, we really needed a yin to Julianne's yang. I knew I wanted a great actress who was funny, dramatic, strong, sexy, over forty, and recognizable. I knew I wasn't going to be able to sit down with anyone in an exploratory way; it was going to be an offer only, so I took the choice very seriously. Julie and I discussed a short list of actresses, and Annette was somebody we both adored. I went out to her [with an offer] and Julie e-mailed her as well, saying, "I'd love for you to do it."

Q: *How was it working with Annette?*

LC: Annette was great and since she was in L.A., we had several script meetings and did some important revisions together. Script work is important to her, and she's good at it. She is formidable—very incisive, smart, and methodical.

This work with Annette prior to Julianne getting to L.A. helped me have a greater understanding of the characters and their relationship. It was critical to helping me be specific in directing them. It allowed me to define the key moments that would translate into relationship authenticity on the screen. Playing the normalcy and humanity of their characters and of their marriage freed them to be natural and steer clear of anything arch and artificial.

SB: Annette was amazing. Every day on set was like an acting clinic. The level of commitment she brought to the character! The homework, the mental and emotional preparation she did. It was an inspiration. I mean, she inhabited the role of Nic.

Q: *How and in what ways did the younger actors surprise you?*

SB: Well, Mia Wasikowska may seem to be one of those "it girls" who's exploded onto the scene, but she's incredibly level-headed and calm. She brought a real centeredness to playing Joni, a real gravitas to this eighteen-year-old. Josh Hutcherson did a wonderful job; he's not at all like Laser in real life. We'd see him go from his own extroverted self to playing someone very internal and almost imploding.

Q: How has the initial feedback been from audiences? The film was first screened in January and February 2010 at the Sundance and Berlin International Film Festivals…

LC: …which I hadn't been preparing to do. We showed it unfinished as a world premiere at Sundance—it was fairly nerve-wracking hustling through temp mixes—but, in spite of that, the film played incredibly well. In fact, the reception was tremendous. The Berlin experience was also incredibly positive.

I think people were relieved to see a film that was grappling with something real and complicated, but was also funny. They've found the honest depiction of marriage and family refreshing, and the gay family aspect takes some audience members into uncharted territory that can be fresh and fun. Viewers at both festivals appreciated the experience—more than I ever anticipated. The movie takes you on a ride that feels truthful and surprising, and drops you off somewhere that is hopeful.

THE KIDS ARE ALL RIGHT

by

Lisa Cholodenko & Stuart Blumberg

```
June 12, 2009 - WHITE
June 24, 2009 - BLUE REVISION
June 30, 2009 - PINK REVISION
August 3, 2009 - GOLDENROD REVISION
```

1   FADE UP ON: 1

    The humming stillness of an American suburb on a summer's
    day: nannies push strollers, joggers jog, mailmen deliver,
    dogs are walked, kids shoot hoop in wide open driveways.

    On a quiet, tree-lined street we pick up two young athletic-
    looking boys riding bikes. LASER ALLGOOD (15) and his
    friend, CLAY (15).

    Like bats out of hell they pass block after block of
    charming, evenly spaced houses until they round a corner and
    drop their bikes in front of a large ranch house.

2   INT. CLAY'S HOUSE - MOMENTS LATER   2

    They walk inside. We HEAR a baseball game on TV in another
    room.

3   INT. CLAY'S, BATHROOM - LATER   3

    Clay pounds on blue pills with a hammer, reducing them to
    powder. Laser watches.

                    LASER
            I don't know, dude.

    Clay cuts the powder into lines with a school ID card.

                    CLAY
            B minus in geometry, yo! This
            shits the bomb!

    Clay rolls up a dollar bill and takes a snort. Then hands
    the rolled up bill to Laser.

                    CLAY (CONT'D)
            Add it up, son.

    Laser takes the bill, bends over and snorts a line.

4   INT. ALLGOOD HOUSE - GIRL'S BEDROOM - DAY   4

    Part Oxford reading room, part teenage girl's lair. Leaning
    against the bed we see JONI ALLGOOD (18). It's her room.
    She pours over a game of Scrabble.

    Sitting next to Joni is her best girl friend, SASHA, (18).
    Sasha's checking out Joni's FACEBOOK PAGE.

Joni's best guy friend, JAI (18) sits across from her, calculating his next Scrabble move.

                    SASHA
          Oh my God, Joni, there are so many
          hotties in your class. You are so
          gonna hook up the first week.

                    JAI
          Just cause you're a 24 hour drive-
          thru doesn't mean everyone else has
          to be...

                    SASHA
          Hey, she worked her ass off! She
          deserves some hot jock sausage!

Jai looks repulsed, and hurt.

                    SASHA (CONT'D)
               (flip)
          Whatever. Why don't you guys just
          do it and get it over with?

Joni and Jai blush. They're both too scared to admit their crush on each other.

                    SASHA (CONT'D)
          What? I'm just asking.

                    JAI
          Uh, maybe because we're friends...

                    SASHA
          Oh, really...?

Sasha turns to Joni like an agent provocateur.

5   INT. CLAY'S HOUSE - TV ROOM - LATER   5

Laser and Clay wrestle on the floor while Clay's DAD watches a baseball game on TV. They bump into the couch. Clay's dad looks back, menacing.

                    CLAY'S FATHER
          Hey, ladies! Take it down a notch.

The boys keep wrestling, wired from the pills. Again, they knock into the couch. Clay's dad spins around, pissed.

                    CLAY'S FATHER (CONT'D)
          What did I just say?!

The Dad grabs Clay, pulls him off of Laser and over the couch. He gets his son in a headlock, forcing the boy's face into his big fat sweaty armpit. Both Dad and Clay enjoy the brutal play. Clay laughs manically.

> CLAY
> Let me go!

> CLAY'S FATHER
> Don't do the crime if you can't do the time.

> CLAY
> Dad, your pits smell like burnt ass! Get off me!

As Laser observes this male-bonding between father and son, we note a trace of longing on his face.

6   OMITTED.   6

7   OMITTED.   7

8   INT. ALLGOOD HOUSE - DINING ROOM   8

Joni, Laser and JULES ALLGOOD (40's) fair-skinned, attractive, sit before well prepared dinner. Still buzzing, Laser taps his fingers incessantly on the table.

> JONI
> Laser! Knock it off!

> LASER
> What?! I'm not doing anything.

9   EXT. HOUSE - ESTABLISHING - MAGIC HOUR   9

NIC ALLGOOD (late 40's) pulls up into the driveway beside a beat up white TRUCK covered in AA slogan bumper stickers.

10   INT. ALLGOOD HOUSE - DINING ROOM - EVENING   10

Nic enters. Drops her bag and heads for the table.

> NIC
> Hi guys. Sorry I'm late.

JULES
Don't worry. We just started.

NIC
27 fibroids. All in the lining.

She kisses Jules.

JULES
Honey, that's disgusting. We're eating.

JONI
Did you do that laparoscopically?

NIC
That's right, Smart Girl. And we got 'em all.

As Nic settles in...

NIC (CONT'D)
Hey, whose truck is that?

JULES
Mine.

NIC
Yours?

JULES
For the business.

NIC
What business?..
(getting edgy)
The gardening?

JONI
(protective)
Isn't it landscaping.

JULES
Yes, thank you very much.

NIC
(strained)
Okay...
(then)
Do we have any Cabarnet left?

JULES
I didn't look, honey.

Nic gets up and goes to the kitchen for wine. Laser's cell phone RINGS. He answers it.

> LASER
> Hey, what's up?

Jules puts her hand on Laser's arm.

> JULES
> Laser, no phone calls at the table.

> LASER
> (into phone)
> Lemme hit you back.

Laser hangs up. Nic re-enters with a large glass of red.

> NIC
> (sitting down)
> Who was that?

> LASER
> Nobody. Clay.

Jules and Nic share a look. Jules starts making maternal windshield wiper strokes with her thumb on Laser's arm.

> JULES
> Can I ask you something? What do you get from your relationship with Clay?

> LASER
> What do you mean, "get"?

Laser looks down at Jules' thumb on his arm.

> JULES
> Do you feel like he's the kind of person who will help you grow?

> LASER
> Mom, you're windshield wiping me.

> NIC
> Hey, did you start on those thank-you notes for your birthday gifts?

> JONI
> Not yet. But I will...

                    NIC
          I just think it's easier to knock
          them out when it's fresh.

                    JONI
          Yeah, I know, I'll do them tonight.

                    NIC
          Great...I mean, you don't want to
          have to start with an apology. You
          know? Then it's embarrassing.

                    JULES
          Okay, honey. She got it. Let it
          go.

                    NIC
          Okay, I'll let it go...
               (then)
          I mean, if it was up to you, our
          kids wouldn't even write thank-you
          notes, they'd just send out good
          vibes.

Nic takes another swig of vino and smiles at Joni through increasingly plum-stained teeth.

                    NIC (CONT'D)
          I can't believe my baby's 18.

                    JULES
          I know...

                    NIC
               (devolving into baby talk)
          Big girl. You're a big girl...

                    JONI
          Mom...

Joni mimes wiping her teeth. Embarrassed, Nic starts licking at her stained teeth.

11   INT. JONI'S BEDROOM - LATER THAT NIGHT   11

       As Joni cranks out thank-you notes, Laser enters.

                    JONI
               What?

       Laser looks nervous.

                    LASER
          Have you thought any more about,
          you know, making that call...?

                    JONI
          Yeah. I don't want to.

                    LASER
          Okay...I was just wondering if you
          changed your mind.

                    JONI
          I haven't.

He starts to leave, but her answer bugs him. He turns back.

                    LASER
          How can you not even be curious?

                    JONI
          Sorry, Laser. I just don't want
          to, okay? I'm leaving soon and I
          don't want to deal with that right
          now.
               (co-dependent leak)
          And also, that could really hurt
          moms' feelings...

                    LASER
          God, why do you worry about them so
          much? They don't even have to know
          about it!

                    JONI
          Look, you can do it when you turn
          18, okay?

                    LASER
          I never ask you for anything.

Laser walks out of the room. Joni feels horrible.

12   INT. NIC AND JULES BEDROOM - THAT NIGHT   12

Nic and Jules lay in bed watching TV, unwinding from the day.

                    NIC
          I just don't understand why you
          bought the truck *now*.

                    JULES
          Because if I'm starting this
          business I need something to haul
          my equipment in.

                    NIC
          Okay. It just seems a little
          cart before the horse.

                    JULES
          What does that mean?

                    NIC
          Sweetie, you don't even have any
          clients yet.

                    JULES
          Well you're the one who's always
          telling me to "act as if!"

                    NIC
               (back peddling)
          That's true. I do. You're right.

The women settle back. Nic sees Jules feels bad.

                    NIC (CONT'D)
          Look, I'm sorry. It's good you
          bought the truck. Its proactive.

Nic caresses Jules' arm, wanting to make it better.

                    NIC (CONT'D)
          Hey...

Jules doesn't look at Nic. She keeps her eyes on the T.V.

                    NIC (CONT'D)
          Wanna watch a movie?

Jules perks up. Nic immediately regrets her suggestion.

                    JULES
          A *movie*-movie?

                    NIC
          Yeah. We haven't done that in a
          while.

MINUTES LATER -- NIC AND JULES

are cozied up side-by-side facing the TV.

ANGLE ON – THE TV

The volume is turned low on TWO NAKED MEN lying on a *chaise longue*. One guy fellating the other.

13   INT. STAIRCASE – SAME   13

Joni tiptoes up a dark staircase and enters an office off the mom's bedroom. She heads for the desk and stealthy opens a drawer. She rummages though with clear intention.

She pulls out a FOLDER and studies the cover. We see the words: *"Pacific Cryo Clinic: Bringing your dreams to life."*

14   INT. BEDROOM – MOMENTS LATER   14

ANGLE ON – THE BED

We now only see Nic. Jules has slipped under the blanket, and is now between Nic's legs. We see Nic trying to get into it, but having a hard time.

                    NIC
          I don't like the guys in this one.
          They're too shaved.

                    JULES
          Don't focus on it.

                    NIC
          How about the one with the biker
          gang?

                    JULES
          We left it in Hawaii.

Jules wrestles with the blankets. Wants them out of her way.

                    NIC
               (pulling them back up)
          I'm cold, honey.

                    JULES
          Sorry. I couldn't breathe.

Jules wrangles the blankets, trying to cover her partner. The transition is awkward and Jules gets caught in the top sheet. As Nic repositions herself, she leans on the VOLUME CONTROL BUTTON and suddenly the porn is blasting at full volume.

                    MAN IN MOVIE
          Suck that fat cock mother-fucker...

                    NIC
          Shit!! Where's the remote?!

                    MAN IN MOVIE
          I'm gonna fuck that tight ass!...

Jules and Nic both dive for the remote. It's lost under the mass of bedding. They struggle to find it as the grunting and 70's disco music blares.

15   INT. OFFICE - JONI   15

Joni turns to the wall, confused. She hears the porno music pulsing though.

16   INT. BEDROOM - MOMENTS LATER   16

Nic finally recovers the remote and hits mute.

                    NIC
          Jesus Christ!

Nic flops back, traumatized.

                    NIC (CONT'D)
          The whole neighborhood heard that!

                    JULES
          No, they didn't.

                    NIC
          Well, *that* was a vibe kill.

Jules looks defeated.

17   INT. OFFICE - MOMENTS LATER   17

Joni turns back to the file on the desk. She flips though some pages of documents and stops. CLOSE ON a PHOTO of a 4 YEAR-OLD BOY standing in a sandbox looking straight into a camera with a big, open grin.

                                               MATCH CUT TO:

18   EXT. FARM - DAY   18

We see that boy, 35 years later, carrying a box of tomatoes and putting them in the back of a truck. This is PAUL, Joni and Laser's biological father.

19   INT. PAUL'S RESTAURANT - "WYSIWYG" - DAY   19

Paul walks in carrying the box of tomatoes. He approaches TANYA, (30's) the restaurant's super sexy hostess.

                    PAUL
          How you doing, foxy?

                    TANYA
          Mm, flapjack, you're smelling ripe.

                    PAUL
          Oh, sorry...

                    TANYA
          No, I like it. It's earthy.

                    PAUL
          What can I say. I've just been out
          there, you know...hoe-ing.
                    (looking at the seating
                     chart)
          How's it looking tonight?

They stand close to each other, peering at the chart.

                    TANYA
          Gonna be tight.

                    PAUL
          Really...

Paul's cell rings. He gives Tanya a hand squeeze and heads for the kitchen, answering.

                    PAUL (CONT'D)
          Hello.

                    WOMAN'S VOICE
          Hi, is this Paul Hatfield?

                    PAUL
          It is. Who's this?

                    WOMAN'S VOICE
          My name is Wendy Minter. I'm
          calling from The Pacific Cryobank.

                    PAUL
          Okay. What can I do for you?

                    WENDY
          I just need to confirm that you
          donated sperm with us between 1991
          and 1993.

At the mention of the word sperm, Paul goes pale.

                    PAUL
          Yeah...I did a little bit of that
          back then...

20   INT. KITCHEN - CONTINUOUS   20

Paul enters. The kitchen is humming with COOKS prepping for
the dinner rush. He looks around for a quiet spot.

                    WENDY
          As you know the Cryobank has a
          confidentiality policy which
          prohibits us from releasing your
          identity without your consent.

A cook, MARGO, approaches Paul to speak with him. Paul nods:
"Can't talk." Hands her the box of tomatoes.

                    PAUL
          Uh-huh.

Paul heads to the back of the kitchen, searching for privacy.

21   INT. PANTRY - SAME   21

Paul moves into the pantry, finds the farthest corner.

                    WENDY (O.S.)
          Well we've been contacted by a
          young woman conceived using your
          semen, and she's asked if you'd be
          open to having contact with her.

Paul's speechless.

22 INT. TANYA'S HOUSE - BEDROOM - NIGHT   22

Paul and Tanya enjoy a hot, sweaty fuck.

23 LATER THAT NIGHT   23

Paul gets dressed while Tanya lays on her messy bed.

                    TANYA
          You must of figured you'd get a
          call at some point.

                    PAUL
          Not really. I mean I was 19 when I
          did it. It was so long ago...I
          just figured no one actually used
          my stuff.

Tanya moves closer to him, flirty.

                    TANYA
          Why? I'd use it.

                    PAUL
              (ignoring the innuendo)
          This is so weird. I mean, a part
          of me's really curious...

                    TANYA
          So what are you gonna do?

                    PAUL
          I don't know.

24 INT. ALLGOOD HOUSE - DINING ROOM   24

Joni and Jules play scrabble at the table. Joni's cell
rings. She grabs it off the counter and answers.

                    JONI
          Hello?

25 EXT. PAUL'S HOUSE - BACK YARD - DAY   25

Paul anxiously paces his overgrown back-yard on his cell
phone. He picks weeds as he talks. <u>Conversation intercut.</u>

PAUL
Hi, I'm looking for Joni Allgood.

JONI
This is she...

PAUL
Hi. This is Paul...
    (clearing his throat)
Uh, your donor...?

JONI
Oh! Hi...

Joni shoots up out of her chair and starts leaving the room to get some privacy away from her mom.

PAUL
Is this a good time to talk?

JONI
    (flustered)
Yeah...

JULES
Where are you going? It's your turn.

Joni doesn't answer. She just walks out to her backyard.

PAUL
So...
    (doesn't know what to say)
How are you?

JONI
I'm good. How are you?

PAUL
I'm well, thanks.

Banal, awkward pause. Paul jumps in to fill the void.

PAUL (CONT'D)
So, Wendy at the Cryobank said you call--

Joni cuts in, nervous and businesslike.

JONI
Actually, my brother asked if I'd
call you because I'm 18 and he's
only 15 which is too young to call--
anyway, he'd like to meet you...if
you want to...

PAUL
(thrown)
Your brother?

JONI
Yeah. Well, technically my half-
brother. Each of my moms had a
kid, you know, with your sperm...

PAUL
No. I didn't know.

JONI
Oh.

PAUL
Both of them?

JONI
Yeah.

PAUL
Like in two?

JONI
Uh huh. Like in gay.

PAUL
Good deal. I love lesbians.

Paul cringes at his lameness. Joni doesn't know what to say.

26   OMITTED.   26

27   EXT. "WYSIWYG", PARKING LOT - NEXT DAY   27

Joni and Laser get out of the car and head to the restaurant
to meet Paul. They're both clearly nervous.

JONI
I just don't want you to have big
expectations.

                    LASER
          Will you quit saying that? I don't
          have any expectations.

                    JONI
          Okay. I'm just saying he
          might be weird. I mean, he donated
          sperm...

                    LASER
          Well if he hadn't done it, you
          wouldn't be here. So respect, yo!

28   INT. "WYSIWYG" - DAY   28

Paul sits alone at a table facing the entrance. He nervously
checks the door as customers enter.

MINUTES LATER-

Joni and Laser enter the restaurant. They look nervous too.

ANGLE ON PAUL

He studies them for a beat, sees them looking around.
Figures they must be "his kids." They look in his direction,
spot him. He raises his hand, stands. They walk over.

The moment is rife. Paul holds out his hand to Joni.

                    PAUL
          Joni. Hey. Nice to meet you.

                    JONI
          Nice to meet you too.

Paul holds out a hand to Laser.

                    PAUL
          And Laser, right?

                    LASER
          Right.

                    PAUL
          Very cool name.

                    LASER
          Thanks.

                    PAUL
          Thanks for making the trek all the
          way over here.

No one knows what comes next.

                    PAUL (CONT'D)
          Cool, I got a table set up for us
          out here...

Paul turns and leads them out to the outdoor dining area.

29   EXT. OUTDOOR DINING AREA - MINUTES LATER   29

They all sit eating. Paul can't help but study their faces.

                    PAUL
          Listen, feel free and ask me
          anything you want, okay?
               (off their stares)
          Or we can just hang out. That's
          fine too. Whatever you guys want.

                    LASER/JONI
          Okay.

Paul presses on, trying to break the ice.

                    PAUL
          Anything you want to ask me, Laser?

                    LASER
          I...uh...I didn't really have any
          specific questions...

                    PAUL
               (helping him out)
          That's fine. I'd love to know
          about you guys. What about you,
          Joni? What are you up to?

                    JONI
          Uh, well, I just graduated high
          school. I'm starting college in
          the fall.

                    PAUL
          Oh yeah? Congratulations.

LASER
Joni's the brains in the family. She won a National Merit Scholarship.

PAUL
Shut the front door!

LASER
Yeah. And she got like an 800 on her Verbal SAT.

JONI
Okay, Laser...

LASER
What? I'm just saying you're really smart.

JONI
No, I just work harder than you.

PAUL
Don't stress it, Laze. School wasn't my thing either and I turned out okay.

LASER
(re: his name)
Laser.

PAUL
I'm sorry. Laser.
(beat)
So tell me about you, Laser. What are you into?

Laser freezes. So his sister jumps in.

JONI
Laser's an amazing athlete.

PAUL
Oh yeah?

LASER
Did you play any sports in school?

PAUL
I played a little basketball in junior high.

                    LASER
          That's it?

                    PAUL
          Pretty much. The whole "team"
          thing got on my nerves, you know
          like, "*Hey, let's go kick some ass,
          man!*" What about you?

                    LASER
          I play some Soccer. Basketball.
          Baseball. You know, team sports.

Paul realizes he's put his foot in his mouth.

                    PAUL
          Hey, I wasn't bagging teams in
          general. Teams are great. I'm
          just weird like that.

                    LASER
          Yeah, I like teams.

We can tell Laser is growing frustrated at his inability to
connect with Paul. Joni jumps in.

                    JONI
          So this is your place?

                    PAUL
          Yeah, I've been working on it for a
          while. I also have this organic co-
          op farm down the road. We use a
          lot of the stuff we grow there for
          the restaurant.

                    JONI
               (excited)
          That's so cool. I'm totally into
          local.

                    LASER
               (busting her)
          You are?

                    JONI
          Uh, yeah Laser! I've been like
          trying to get moms to buy local for
          forever.

Laser tries again to reconnect.

                    LASER
          So, like, do you raise pigs and
          stuff?

                    PAUL
          No. No pigs...
               (beat)
          But it's a great spot. You guys
          should come check it out sometime.

                    JONI
          Yeah...Definitely...

Excited, Joni turns to Laser. He seems uninterested.

30   EXT. WYSIWYG, PARKING LOT - DAY   30

The kids and Paul exit the restaurant. Paul walks to a
classic BMW motorcycle. Lasers tries to hide his awe.

                    LASER
          Is that yours?

                    PAUL
          Yeah. You like motorcycles?

                    LASER
          Yeah, but...our moms are kind of
          anti-motorcycle.

                    JONI
          And by "kind of" he means they'd
          kill us if we ever rode one.

                    PAUL
          That's too bad. They're fun.

Time to say goodbye. Again, no one knows the protocol here.
After an awkward beat, Paul holds out his arms for hugs.

                    PAUL (CONT'D)
          Well it was great to meet you guys.

He and Joni hug.

                    PAUL (CONT'D)
          I hope this was okay.

                    JONI
          Yeah...totally...thank you.

Now Paul and Laser share a somewhat awkward man-hug.

                    PAUL
          Really nice to meet you, Laser.

                    LASER
          Yeah.

Joni gives a quick wave to Paul. She turns to go and Laser
follows. Paul watches them walk away. He looks stirred up
by the meeting.

31   INT. JONI'S CAR - DAY   31

Joni and Laser head back home.

                    JONI
          I just never pictured him that way.
          I just...I don't know...He was so
          cool and interesting. I can't
          believe that was him...He was so
          nice, you know?...

                    LASER
          I guess...

                    JONI
          You guess?

                    LASER
          Yeah...

                    JONI
          God, Laser! You're the one that
          wanted to meet him so bad!

                    LASER
          I know.

                    JONI
          Well what did you think of him?

                    LASER
          I don't know. He seemed kind of
          into himself.

32   OMITTED   32

33   INT. ALLGOOD HOUSE - TV ROOM - LATER THAT NIGHT   33

Nic and Jules are cuddled up affectionately on the couch watching cable. They see Laser on his way out of the house.

                    JULES
          Hey bug, come here. We're watching
          "Locked Up Abroad: Uganda."

                    LASER
          I saw it. It was gnarly.

                    NIC
          Where are you going?

                    LASER
          Clay's.

Jules and Nic shoot each other a concerned look.

                    NIC
          Don't be back late, okay?

                    LASER
          I know.

                    JULES
          Can I have a hug before you go?

                    LASER
          Mom...

                    JULES
          Just a quick one. Please!

                    LASER
          Hug her. That's what she's there
          for.

Laser leaves. Nic hits mute on the TV, looks at Jules.

                    NIC
          Ugh. Maybe we should just sit him
          down and ask him already.

                    JULES
          What? "Are you and Clay fucking?"

                    NIC
          "Exploring" is the word I'd use...

                    JULES
          And what if he is "exploring?"
          This is the age for that. Why
          should we care?

                    NIC
          We shouldn't...
               (then)
          I just don't understand why he's
          exploring with that loser.

                    JULES
          Look, we don't even know what the
          deal is. We're jumping to
          conclusions.

                    NIC
          I feel like he has so much
          potential and he's just wasting it.

Nic's comment hits a nerve in Jules.

                    JULES
          What are you trying to say?

                    NIC
          What do you mean, what am I trying
          to say?

                    JULES
          It feels like there's some subtext
          here.

                    NIC
          What are you talking about?

                    JULES
          I don't know: Like mother like son?
          Is that it? Both of us aimless,
          wandering in the darkness, "wasting
          our potential?"

Nic won't go there.

                    NIC
          Okay, honey, you're on a whole
          other tangent and I have no idea
          what you're talking about.

                    JULES
          Well, maybe it hasn't risen to the
          plane of consciousness for you yet.

                    NIC
          Yeah. Maybe not.

Nic clicks the volume back on, freezing Jules out.

34   INT. PAUL'S RESTAURANT - AFTERNOON   34

Paul and Tanya sit at the bar, eating family-meal.

                    TANYA
          So what were they like?

                    PAUL
          Sweet. They were really good kids.
          The boy's kind of a sensitive jock
          and the girl's kind of innocent but
          whip-smart and super cute.

                    TANYA
          Sounds like you connected.

                    PAUL
          Yeah, we kinda did.

                    TANYA
          Where'd you leave it?

                    PAUL
          We didn't really leave it anywhere.

Brooke, the sexy Wiccan volunteer, comes up to Paul bearing a basket of freshly-picked fruits.

                    BROOKE
          Hey Paul.

Paul leans over the basket.

                    PAUL
          Whatcha got? Oh cool. First
          strawberries of the season.

                    BROOKE
          Don't they look awesome? I thought
          you should have the first taste.

And with that, she smiles, hands him the basket and leaves.

                    TANYA
              (mimicking Brooke)
         "I thought you should have the
         first taste...of my pussy."

Paul can't help smiling at the nasty talk.

                    PAUL
         Whoa...

35   INT. NIC AND JULES BEDROOM - AFTERNOON   35

Clay rummages through the top drawer of Jules' dresser.
Laser stands behind him, uncomfortable.

                    LASER
         Dude, I don't think they smoke pot.

                    CLAY
         Hold up.

Clay freezes. CLOSE ON a row of sex toys including a fancy
pink, Japanese "all-in-one" dildo and a few DVD's.

                    CLAY (CONT'D)
         Whoa!

Clay turns on the dildo. It starts to gyrate.

                    CLAY (CONT'D)
         Yo, it's alive!

                    LASER
         Dude, put it back!!

Laughing, Clay throws the dildo back in the drawer. Then he
grabs one of the DVDs and spins back around.

                    CLAY
         Dude, we're watching this.

36   INT. LASER'S ROOM - DAY   36

Laser and Clay sit on the bed. They look at each other.
Then Laser hits play.

ON SCREEN

We see a COP giving a young MAN a BLOW-JOB. Laser and Clay
sit motionless, shocked, disgusted, riveted.

                              CLAY
                Think the whole thing's like this?

                              LASER
                Want me to fast-forward?

Clay doesn't answer. They just keep watching.

37   OMITTED   37

38   OMITTED   38

39   EXT. ALLGOOD HOUSE - DRIVEWAY - DAY   39

        Jules pulls her truck into the driveway, almost running over
        Laser's bike.

40   INT. LASER'S ROOM - DAY   40

        Laser and Clay are still watching the porn...<u>as Jules walks
        in the room</u>.

                              JULES
                Laser, you left your bike out...

        Laser reflexively grabs for the remote. As he fumbles for
        it, Jules sees what they're watching. She looks mortified.

41   INT. ALLGOOD HOUSE - KITCHEN - THAT EVENING   41

        We enter a family conference already in progress.

        Nic and Jules act calm but are inwardly mortified that their
        15-year-old son found their porn.

                              NIC
                Laser, your mom and I accept you
                and love you unconditionally? You
                know that, right?

                              LASER
                Yeah.

                              NIC
                And you know you can be open with
                us about anything.

                    LASER
          Yeah, I know.

Jules steels herself for a frank discussion.

                    JULES
          Laser, is there anything you want
          to talk about?

                    LASER
          Like what?

                    NIC
          Anything. Anything on your mind.

Laser cracks his knuckles.

                    LASER
          Well there is something.

Nic and Jules share a look. "Here we go."

                    LASER (CONT'D)
          It's more of a question, really.

                    NIC
          That's okay.

                    JULES
          We won't judge you.

Laser looks at his moms. Nic and Jules brace themselves.

                    LASER
          Why do you guys watch gay man-porn?

Nic and Jules look at each other, thrown.

                    NIC
          Well, first I have to say we rarely
          watch that movie--

Jules touches Nic's arm.

                    JULES
          Honey...

                    NIC
          And secondly, I really don't
          appreciate you snooping around our
          room. Was that Clay's idea? I
          have to say again, I don't like
          him. He seems untended...!

JULES
Honey, that's not what he asked--

NIC
(snapping)
Fine. Do you want to answer his question?!

JULES
Well, sweetie, human sexuality is complicated. And sometimes, people's desires can be...counter-intuitive...
(soldiering on)
For instance, since women's sexual responsiveness is mostly internal, sometimes it's exciting for us to see sexual responsiveness more, you know...
(beat)
...externalized.

Laser looks at them, still baffled.

JULES (CONT'D)
Like with a penis.

LASER
But like, wouldn't you rather watch two women doing it?

JULES
You would think that. But in most of those movies, they've hired two straight women to pretend and the inauthenticity is just unbeara--

NIC
Okay, that's enough! Laser, your mom and I have a sense there's some other stuff going on in your life and we just want to be let in.

LASER
What do you mean?

JULES
Are you having a relationship with someone?

NIC
You could tell us, honey. We'd understand and support you.

Laser looks confused. How did they find out about Paul?

                    LASER
          I just met him once.

Nic and Jules share a worried look.

                    NIC
          What do you mean once?

                    JULES
          Did he find you on-line?!

                    LASER
          What?!

                    NIC
          Who did you meet once?

                    LASER
          Paul! I met him with Joni.

                    NIC
          Who's Paul?!

                    JULES
          Why was Joni there?!

                    LASER
          She set it up.

                    NIC
          Forget the set-up! Who is Paul?!!

                    LASER
          Our sperm donor.

Jules and Nic go white.

                    LASER (CONT'D)
          Wait, did you guys think I was
          gay?!

42   INT. ALLGOOD HOUSE - LIVING ROOM - LATER   42

Joni has been pulled into the family conference. Nic and Jules are trying to remain as calm as possible. Nic slugs a gulp of wine.

                    JULES
          Look, guys, we understand why you'd
          be curious about your biological
          father. That's totally natural.

                    NIC
          But why didn't you tell us?

                    JONI
          Because we knew you'd be upset.

                    NIC
          WE'RE NOT UPSET!!

Jules calms her riled-up partner.

                    JULES
          Honey...
                (to Joni; expressing her
                 upset more calmly)
          We just wish you'd have included us
          in your thinking. But what's done
          is done. You met him, and now you
          guys can move on--

                    JONI
                (sheepish)
          Actually...
                (beat)
          I want to see him again.

          JULES   LASER
You do?!   You do?!

                    JONI (CONT'D)
                (to Laser)
          Yeah. I was gonna tell you.

                    NIC
          Whoa! Whoa! No. No way.
                (regaining dominance)
          Nobody is seeing anyone until *we*
          meet him!

Joni looks at Laser. They knew this would happen.

43   INT. NIC AND JULES' BATHROOM - NIGHT   43

Nic and Jules do a post-mortem as they floss.

NIC
Yeah, I get it. He's their biological father and all that crap but it still feels really shitty. Like we're not enough or something, you know?

JULES
Of course I know. I don't want to time-share our kids with someone. Especially when it's Joni's last summer home. No way.

When Jules leaves the room Nic pulls a clump of long, wet red hair out of the sink.

NIC
Jesus, Jules! The plumber was just here!

Nic throws the clump of hair in the trash.

44 INT. NIC AND JULES BEDROOM - MOMENTS LATER 44

NIC
(getting tactical)
Look, we need to be smart about this. If we act like grubby bitches, we're just gonna make it worse.

JULES
I know...

NIC
Let's just kill him with kindness and put it to bed.

JULES
I'm with you, honey.
(then)
We're gonna get through this, okay?

Nic smiles. She loves when Jules shows confidence.

NIC
I love you, chicken.

The women bump fists. They have a plan.

JULES
I love you too, pony.

| 45 | EXT. STREET - AFTERNOON | 45 |

Paul rides slowly down the street, checking addresses. He pulls over and cuts his engine in front of the Allgood house.

| 46 | OMITTED | 46 |

| 47 | INT/EXT. ALLGOOD FRONT DOOR - AFTERNOON | 47 |

Paul rings the bell. Waits. The door opens and Nic and Jules are there smiling with "kill him with kindness" faces.

NIC
Paul! It is so great to meet you.
I'm Nic. This is Jules.

Paul shakes their hands.

PAUL
Hi, great to meet you two.

JULES
I hope the traffic wasn't too bad.

PAUL
No, I've got my bike so...I just sort of weave through.

Nic clocks the motorcycle, stifles the impulse to judge.

NIC
Great. Well, come on in.

As they enter, Paul holds out a bottle of wine.

PAUL
This is for you. I don't know if you guys like wine...

Nic takes it.

NIC
Are you kidding? We love it.
(checking the label)
And a Petit Syrah. What a treat!
Let me get some glasses.

Nic leaves Paul by the stairs with Jules. Little silence. Jules steals a look at him, unable to contain her curiosity.

PAUL
Beautiful house. How long you guys lived here?

JULES
Almost ten years. Wait, has it been that long?
(rambling nervously)
We moved right after Laser broke his leg, I remember that because we had a ramp for a while, so that would have been...ten, no, nine? No, ten years this fall.

Paul nods, smiling at her nervousness.

PAUL
Okay.

Laser and Joni enter. Joni lights up when she sees Paul. Jules watches Paul hug her. Uncomfortable, she heads for

THE KITCHEN --

Jules finds Nic's pouring herself a sizable glass of wine.

JULES
You okay?

NIC
(not okay)
Yeah. Fine.

Jules feels her inner co-dependent swelling in her chest.

JULES
Go easy on the wine, hon. It's day time.

NIC
Okay. And same goes for the micro-managing...

48 EXT. ALLGOOD PORCH - AFTERNOON 48

Everyone sits at the picnic table.

JULES
I hope the food's okay. Joni told us you own a restaurant.

PAUL
The food's great. Can't go wrong with salmon and corn.

Nic finishes a glass of wine as Jules takes note.

NIC
So Paul, did you always know you wanted to be in food-services industry?

Paul smiles at Nic, trying to disarm her.

PAUL
Well, I always liked food.

NIC
No, I was asking because I remember reading in your file, back when we were looking for, you know, *sperm,* anyway, you said you were studying international relations.

PAUL
Oh yeah. Wow, that was a long time ago. Yeah, I was considering it, but then I dropped out of school.

JONI
You dropped out of college?

PAUL
Yeah, it wasn't my thing.

NIC
(squinching)
No? Why's that?

PAUL
It just seemed like a massive waste of money after a while. I mean, I wasn't "doing" anything. I was just sitting on my ass listening to people spout off ideas I could've just as easily learned reading a book.

Paul sees that his little rant may be alienating the moms.

PAUL (CONT'D)
I'm not saying higher learning uniformly sucks. I mean, college is great for some people.
(MORE)

PAUL (CONT'D)
Joni, I'm sure you're gonna love it. That's just me. I'm just weird that way.
(beat)
Which is probably why I ended up in the food-services industry.

LASER
See what he did there, mom? You said "food-services industry," then he said "food-services industry..."

NIC
Yeah, I got it, Laser. Thanks.
(apropos of nothing)
So, Paul, what about your social life?

PAUL
My social life?

NIC
You know, are you married, divorced, seeing anyone?

JONI
Mom!

NIC
What? We're getting to know Paul.

PAUL
No, never been married or divorced. I date a little, but I'm just kind of focused on my work right now.

NIC
Oh.

Paul wants a break from the heat.

PAUL
So, how'd you guys meet?

Jules smiles, embarrassed. Nic jumps in.

NIC
We met at UCLA. I was a resident in the ER and Jules had an emergency.

JULES
My tongue went numb.

PAUL
Really?

THUD! We turn to see Laser, pounding his head on the table.

JULES
Laser, that's not nice.

LASER
What's not nice is subjecting your kids to the same story 1000 times!

PAUL
(ignoring Laser)
What happened to your tongue?

JULES
I don't know. I just lost all the feeling in my face and tongue and I thought I might gag and then, you know...

PAUL
Choke? Die?...

JULES
Yeah...exactly...

NIC
Well it was pretty clear to me she was just having an anxiety attack and she'd be fine.

PAUL
So what'd you do for her?

NIC
Gave her a Vallium. Tried to get her to relax, talk, move her tongue around.

LASER
Mom, that's gross!

JULES
(ignoring Laser, to Nic)
Actually, she started teasing me and that really helped.

NIC
I was trying to distract you.

JULES
I know. And it worked. You were really funny.

NIC
You were really pretty.

Nic reaches over and caresses Jules' hand. Joni rolls her eyes, embarrassed.

JULES
So that's it. My tongue started working again.

NIC
And we've been glued at the hip ever since.

PAUL
That's a great story.

JULES
(beaming)
We like it.

Laser and Joni share a look.

PAUL
So Nic, I know you're a doctor. How 'bout you, Jules? What do you do?

Jules never likes this question.

JULES
Well, I, you know, I studied architecture in college...

PAUL
Right...

JULES
But I'm not an architect. I mean I was on my way to becoming one. But I quit before the kids were born.

PAUL
Well, that happens...

JULES
When they got a little older, I started a Balinese furniture import business...

                    PAUL
Right on.

                    JULES
Yeah. But that didn't work out.

                    PAUL
Well, business aren't easy--

                    JULES
Actually, I'm in the process of
starting a new business.

                    PAUL
Good for you. What kind?

                    JULES
Landscape design...
          (before he can respond)
But not like a gardener! I mean,
yes, there's a gardening component
to it, but the real work is to
create unique, eco-friendly outdoor
spaces that harmonize with the
surrounding environment. Do you
know what I mean?

                    PAUL
Absolutely.

In Nic's mind, Jules is drowning in verbiage. So she jumps
in to save her.

                    NIC
Hey Paul, did Joni tell you about
her graduation speech?

                    PAUL
No, she didn't.

                    NIC
It was incredible. So full of
wisdom and hope...
          (turning to her Joni)
Hon, go get it. I'm sure he'd love
to hear it...

                    JONI
          (blushing)
No, mom, I'm sure he wouldn't...

                    NIC
          Sure he would. Come on. Go get
          it...

                    JONI
               (getting upset)
          No, it's okay...

                    NIC
          Sweetie, don't be embarrassed.

                    JONI
          I'm not embarrassed! Jesus! Give
          it a rest already!

This outburst stuns Nic into silence. Her daughter has never
spoken to her like this. Laser stands up.

                    LASER
          I'll get the ice-cream.

                    JONI
               (standing up)
          I'll help you.

Joni and Laser leave the room. Nic pours herself the last of
Paul's Petit Syrah. Jules smiles, covering her anxiety.

                    JULES
               (softly)
          Honey, that's your forth glass.

                    NIC
          Actually, it's my third. But
          thanks for counting.

Paul turns to Jules, trying to revive the mood.

                    PAUL
          Hey, I was just thinking. You
          know, I bought this place last year
          and the backyard's a wreck. Would
          you be interested in working on it?

                    JULES
               (insecure)
          Oh, that's okay.

                    PAUL
          No, seriously. I don't have time
          to work on it myself.

                    JULES
          Thank you. That's really sweet.
          Why don't you think about it.

                    PAUL
          Why? I just did.
               (then)
          I mean, if you're not up for it
          that's okay--

                    JULES
               (jumping on it)
          No! I am!
               (getting excited)
          I'm up for it!...

Jules smiles at Nic: "Isn't this great? My first client."
Nic looks less than pleased.

49   OMITTED.   49

50   INT. HARDWARE STORE - DAY   50

Nic pushes a cart piled high with gardening supplies. Jules
grabs a couple BAGS of fertilizer, throws them on top.

                    NIC
          ...I'm just saying, the plan was to
          limit his involvement--

                    JULES
          You're unbelievable. You're all
          over me about getting clients, I
          finally get one and you're--

                    NIC
          He's not just a *client*, Jules.
          He's our sperm donor! Have you
          ever heard the phrase "Don't Shit
          Where You Eat?"

                    JULES
          Yes, and I think it's disgusting.

The two separate, go down separate isles. When they rejoin,
Nic is contrite.

                    NIC
          I'm sorry. He just seemed sort
          of...self-satisfied to me.

Jules grabs the olive branch.

                    JULES
Yeah, he was working the whole "alternative" thing pretty hard.

                    NIC
        (mimicking)
"I just need to get outside and 'do' things, not sit on my ass and *learn*. But that's just me. I'm weird that way."

They both laugh. Nic's funny sometimes.

51   EXT. PAUL'S HOUSE - ECHO PARK - DAY   51

Jules drives slowly up the hill looking for Paul's address. She sees the house and pulls in the driveway next to an old truck and a motorcycle.

52   EXT. PAUL'S HOUSE - BACK YARD - DAY   52

Jules and Paul walk through Paul's backyard, evaluating.

                    JULES
...We could do a kind of a Secret Garden thing with trellises and topiary...
        (clocking his face)
...or something more Asian, minimal, with a rock garden feel. It's up to you...

                    PAUL
What do you think?

                    JULES
Personally, I'm tired of minimal. I'm into more is more. Let's not try to tame the space. I think it would look great all lush and overgrown and fecund...

                    PAUL
Fecund?

                    JULES
I'm sorry, you know, fertile...

                    PAUL
          No, I love that word. You just
          don't hear it that often.
               (thinking)
          More is more. Yeah. Let's do that.

Jules is staring at Paul.

                    PAUL (CONT'D)
          What?

                    JULES
          Sorry, I just keep seeing my kids
          in your expressions...

Jules looks more intensely at Paul's face.

                    JULES (CONT'D)
          You and Laser have the same mouth.

                    PAUL
          You think so?

                    JULES
          Yeah.

The observation strikes Paul. Suddenly, he's feeling a kind of fast-tracked intimacy with Jules he hadn't expected.

53   EXT. BACKYARD - ALLGOOD HOUSE - EVENING   53

Jules and Laser play Ping-Pong as Nic gets home with Chinese take-out for the family dinner.

                    NIC
          What's the score?

                    JULES
          Pretty close.

Laser cranks a forehand that whizzes past Jules.

                    LASER
          20-3...match point.

                    NIC
          So how'd it go today?

                    JULES
          Great. We settled on a concept.

                         NIC
               What is it?

                         JULES
               It's hard to explain. You have to
               kind of see the space to get it.

                         NIC
                    (to Laser)
               Laser, did you write Pup-pup a Get
               Well card?
                    (off his silence)
               Laser! What do I have to do?! I
               bought you a card. I left it on
               your desk. All you had to do was--

                         LASER
               Mom, settle! I will...

                         NIC
               Don't tell me to settle, mister.
               And if it's not in the mail by
               tomorrow morning, we're not going
               to the Dodger game Saturday.

                         LASER
               Whatever, I have other plans
               anyway.

                         NIC
               What other plans?
                    (off his silence)
               I'm asking you a quest--

                         LASER
               I said I'd do something with Paul!

Laser serves a rocket, whizzing past a flailing Jules. He
tosses the racquet on the table and leaves. Nic yells:

                         NIC
               You used to be so cute!

54   EXT. ALLEY - DAY   54

We cut onto Paul and Laser, looking out at something. Laser
is holding a DIGITAL VIDEO CAMERA.

                         PAUL
               This may not be a good idea.

                    CLAY (O.S.)
          Are you filming?!

We cut to Clay on a skateboard on the ledge of a brick wall.
He's preparing to ride the ledge, jump a dumpster and land
his board on the ground.

                    PAUL
              (to Laser)
          He's not gonna make it.
              (calling to Clay)
          Clay, you're not gonna make it!

                    LASER
          I think he may be right, dude.
          Maybe this isn't such a good idea.

                    CLAY
          Will you quit being a man-gina and
          run the camera! I'm only doing
          this once so keep my shit in frame!

Laser sighs, then holds up the camera. Paul looks at Laser,
wondering why he puts up with this guy.

VIDEO CAMERA'S POV: We watch as Clay psychs himself up with
an assortment of deep breaths and head-slaps. Finally, he
starts down the ledge. He starts his jump, catches air and
hits the edge of the dumpster and falls. We see him go into
the dumpster and land with a nauseating THUD. Paul and Laser
rush up and look over the edge.

                    PAUL/LASER
          ARE YOU OKAY?!

There's Clay, his arm bent at a disturbing angle, in agony.

                    CLAY
          Did you get that?!

                    LASER
          Seriously, dude, are you okay?

                    CLAY
          I'm fucking fine! Fuck! Did you
          fucking get it?!

EXT. STREET OUTSIDE CLAY'S HOUSE - LATER

Paul and Laser walk over to Paul's truck.

PAUL
Maybe next time we can hang out just you and me.

LASER
Clay's cool. He's just gets a little amped sometimes.

PAUL
That's not amped. That's being a dick.

LASER
He's not a dick, that's just his way.

PAUL
Okay...I just didn't like the way he was talking to you.

LASER
(defensive)
Well, you don't know him.

PAUL
(back-peddling)
You're right...I don't...

LASER
Hey, can I ask you a question?

PAUL
Sure.

LASER
Why'd you donate sperm?

PAUL
Well, it's a lot more fun then donating blood.

Laser doesn't laugh. Paul realizes he's gonna have to give a "non-joke" answer.

PAUL (CONT'D)
I don't know, I guess I thought, you know, if I can help somebody in need, somebody who wants a baby...

Laser's not really buying that.

LASER
So you did it to help people?

                    PAUL
          It was a long time ago...

                    LASER
          How much did you get paid?

                    PAUL
          Why do you want to know?

                    LASER
          I'm just curious.

                    PAUL
          I don't know, like 60 bucks a pop.

                    LASER
          That's it?

                    PAUL
          It was worth more back then. You
          know. With inflation...
               (off Laser's look)
          Hey, I'm glad I did it...

Laser doesn't quite buy Paul's altruism. He looks over at him, then away.

56   INT. JONI'S ROOM - DAY   56

Jai and Joni and Sasha play Scrabble. Sasha checks out the photos of Paul on Joni's phone.

                    SASHA
          Hello? Donor Dad? Stone cold fox.

                    JAI
          Must you take everything beautiful
          and make it dirty?

                    SASHA
          I'm just saying. Spermster's a
          hottie. Is he single?

                    JONI
          Okay, first of all, ewww. Second,
          he's a really good person and I'd
          prefer it if you didn't taint him
          with your whore juice.

Sasha hops up, energized by the banter.

                    SASHA
          Fair enough, hairy muff. I'm outta
          here. You love birds can split my
          letters...

Sasha splits and suddenly the room is thick with nervous
tension.

                    JONI
          You want to keep playing?

                    JAI
          Sure.

As Jai incorporates Sasha's tiles into his own, we see Joni
gathering her nerve to make a move. Jai probably feels it
but in his nervousness he can't look at Joni.

                    JAI (CONT'D)
          Sometimes I feel sorry for Sasha,
          you know...

                    JONI
          Yeah...

Joni starts to move in, her face draws closer to Jai's, inch
by inch.

Somehow, deep down, Jai can sense her moving towards him
which exhilarates and freaks the shit out of him at the same
time. To the point where he lets slip...

                    JAI
          It's like she has to sexualize
          every experience, you know? It's
          just sad...

That stops Joni in her tracks.

                    JONI
          Yeah, it is. It's really sad.

Jai's sabotaged the mood and they both know it.

57   INT. NIC AND JULES' BATHROOM - NIGHT   57

Jules walks in to find Nic in sexy satin man-PJ's, sitting at
the rim of a RUNNING BATH. There are candles burning.

                    JULES
          Wow. What's this?

NIC
Come here. Sit down.

Jules takes a seat beside her. Nic holds her hand.

NIC (CONT'D)
I'm sorry I've been such a bitch lately. I know I'm not being my highest self.

JULES
Yeah, well...

NIC
You've been really patient with me. I just want you to know that hasn't gone unrecognized.

Nic gives her a long, sweet kiss. Jules is warming up.

NIC (CONT'D)
Get in.

CUT TO - JULES

In the tub, revelling in the warm bubbly water. Nic is sitting on the ledge, massaging her feet.

JULES
Oh god, chicken, that's the spot.

NIC
How's the water?

JULES
Perfect. You wanna come in?

NIC
In a bit. You enjoy it first.

Nic goes deeper with the massage. Jules' eyes roll back.

NIC (CONT'D)
Oh, I forgot the lavender salts.

Nic starts to get up. Jules grabs her hand.

JULES
No, don't stop...

NIC
No, I meant to put 'em in....

Nic gets up and sashays to the door.

                    NIC (CONT'D)
          Don't move...

Nic exits. Jules sinks back, wishing Nic had stayed.

58   CUT TO JULES - MINUTES LATER   58

Still waiting. Getting impatient and upset.

                    JULES
          Nic?!!

No response.

CUT TO THE KITCHEN --

Nic is on her cell with a patient, a glass of wine in her hand. Jules walks in wearing a bathrobe. Nic turns. Raises a finger and mouths: "Sorry..."

                    NIC
          No, we're planning on being here
          through mid-August so...
               (beat)
          No, I promise, I'm not going
          anywhere.

Jules' face drops; she turns and leaves.

59   OMITTED.   59

60   INT./EXT. PAUL'S HOUSE - DAY   60

Paul watches Jules work in his backyard. Luis hauls shrubs.

61   INT. PAUL'S HOUSE - KITCHEN - LATER   61

Paul and Jules stand at the kitchen table, looking over her sketch for the yard.

                    JULES
          Look, I'm gonna go to the nursery
          in the morning so we should
          probably make sure you're signed
          off on the Bougainvillea...

Jules looks over at a pan on the kitchen counter.

                    JULES (CONT'D)
          What's that?

                    PAUL
          Strawberry rhubarb pie. Fresh from
          my garden.

Paul hands her a fork and she takes a big bite. Her eyes
roll back in her head.

                    PAUL (CONT'D)
          Good, huh?

                    JULES
          Oh my god. That is criminal.

                    PAUL
          Have more.

                    JULES
          No, please, just take it away...

                    PAUL
          You had one bite.

                    JULES
          I have another you may as well just
          tape it to my ass cause that's
          where it'll end up.

                    PAUL
          Hey now, don't go negative on your
          ass.

Jules blushes at all this talk of her ass.

                    JULES
          So...you're good with the plants?
               (off his silence)
          Look, we don't have to do that. We
          could do go in a totally different
          direction if you--

                    PAUL
          No, I'm just thinking. Hang on.
               (covers his eyes)
          Yeah, I'm good with the plants.

                    JULES
          Sorry. Sometimes I mistake silence
          for criticism.

PAUL
I wasn't criticizing you.

JULES
No, I know...I just...
(beat)
Sometimes Nic can be a little critical, you know. She's a perfectionist.

PAUL
That doesn't mean you have to be negative.

Jules looks away. We HEAR a knock from the back.

LUIS (O.S.)
Excuse me, Senora? Hello?

Jules turns, sees Luis standing at the glass door.

JULES
What's up?

LUIS
5 o'clock.

JULES
Yeah. Okay.

Jules wants Luis to leave her alone. But he's not going.

LUIS
Same time tomorrow?

JULES
Yes! Same time!

Luis leaves. Jules turns back to Paul, laughs nervously.

JULES (CONT'D)
Okay. I'm gonna take off too...

PAUL
(in Luis's accent)
Same time tomorrow?

Jules pushes Paul, laughing.

JULES
That's mean.

Paul hands her a Tupperware with some of the pie in it.

                    PAUL
          Here, take this...

                    JULES
          No!

                    PAUL
          Just give it to the kids.

                    JULES
          Okay! God, you're such a pusher!

Jules grabs the pie and gives him a kiss on the mouth, almost
as a mistake. Before they know it, they're making out.

Jules snaps back, freaked.

                    JULES (CONT'D)
          Whoa. I'm sorry. That was...I
          don't know where that came from...

                    PAUL
               (freaked himself)
          It's okay...

                    JULES
          Okay. I'm gonna go now...

Jules starts backing away, acting as if nothing happened.

                    PAUL
          Jules...?

                    JULES
               (overcompensating)
          ...but I shall return!

Jules bolts for the door, clutching her pie. Paul watches
her go, stunned by what just happened.

62   INT. NIC AND JULES BEDROOM - NIGHT   62

Nic's in bed reading a magazine. Jules gets in bed,
paranoid. Nic puts her magazine down.

                    NIC
          So how'd it go with Paul?

                    JULES
               (jumpy)
          What do you mean?

                    NIC
          I don't know. Did you break
          ground? Did you dig in? I don't
          know the terms.

                    JULES
          No, we just talked...conceptually.

                    NIC
          Oh, so it was less of a "doing"
          day, huh? Was he okay with that?

                    JULES
          You know, maybe we should lay off
          the Paul digs a little.

                    NIC
          Okay. You're right.

Chastened, Nic looks back at her magazine. Jules rolls over.

                    JULES
          And I also think we should start
          composting.

63   OMITTED   63

64   EXT. URBAN FARM - ECHO PARK - DAY - MOS   64

Sweating and dirty, Joni and Paul pull radishes from the
ground. They're in a zone together. Paul takes off his sun-
hat and put it on Joni's head.

                    PAUL
          You got your mom's fair skin. You
          didn't get my Mediterranean
          genes...

                    JONI
          Thanks...

Joni's cell rings. She looks. Rolls her eyes.

                    JONI (CONT'D)
          Ugh. Ignore.

Joni hits the ignore button, puts her cell away.

                    PAUL
          Who's that?

                    JONI
          My mom, Nic. She's making me
          insane.

                    PAUL
          Why? What's she doing?

                    JONI
          She's treating me like I'm 12.
          It's like she doesn't want to admit
          I'm an adult.

                    PAUL
          She's your mom. That's her job.

                    JONI
          What? To smother me to death?
          That's not her job.

                    PAUL
          Well, if you want things to be
          different, *you've* got to make that
          happen. That's *your* job.

65   EXT. SUBURBAN STREET - MAGIC HOUR   65

Laser walks with Clay. Clay sports a homemade arm-cast for the skateboard mishap we witnessed earlier.

                    CLAY
          That jump was cake, dude! I so
          could've made it.

                    LASER
          You were like 20 feet short, dude!
          There was no way.

                    CLAY
          Yeah, well if Paul wasn't there I
          could have landed it. That guy
          creeps me out.

                    LASER
          Whatever.

                    CLAY
          He's kind of a fag, dude. Tryin'
          to act all like your dad and shit.

Laser doesn't know how to respond so he ignores the comment. A stray DOG comes up to them. Laser stops to pet it.

                    LASER
          Hey buddy. Good boy.

Laser sees the dog has no tags. He looks around for an
owner. The dog nuzzles Laser for affection.

                    LASER (CONT'D)
          I've seen this dog around. I
          wonder if he's lost.

                    CLAY
          Let's pee on his head.

                    LASER
          What?

Clay unzips his fly. It's difficult with the plaster cast.

                    LASER (CONT'D)
          Dude, don't do that.

                    CLAY
          Come on. Hold him...

Clay yanks the dog by his scruff.

                    LASER
          Dude, Quit it!

                    CLAY
               (mocking)
          Duuude, quit it!

Suddenly, Laser gets it. His friend is the tool. He grabs
the dog and smacks him to get him to run away.

                    LASER
          Go! Run! Get out of here!

The dog TAKES OFF. Clay shoves Laser.

                    CLAY
          Why are you such a fag?!

Laser shoves Clay back hard.

                    LASER
          Why are you such a dick?!

Clay HITS Laser in the mouth. Laser touches his lip. Sees
blood, and walks away. Friendship over.

66   EXT. URBAN FARM PARKING LOT - ECHO PARK - MAGIC HOUR   66

Paul and Joni walk to his motorcycle parked in the dirt lot behind them. Paul grabs his helmet off the bike, hands it to Joni.

> PAUL
> Here, put this on.

Joni takes the helmet and puts it on. Paul fastens the buckle for her. They get on the bike and take off down the hill.

67   EXT. ECHO PARK TO THE WEST SIDE - MAGIC HOUR   67

Paul takes Joni home on his motorcycle via Sunset Boulevard. She holds Paul tightly.

68   INT. ALLGOOD HOUSE - LIVING ROOM - EVENING   68

The ladies sit in the living room watching TV.

> JULES
> Relax. She'll get home when she gets home.

> NIC
> Quit telling me to relax!

They go back to watching TV. After a beat, we HEAR a motorcycle pull up.

> NIC (CONT'D)
> What the fuck...!

69   EXT. ALLGOOD HOUSE - CONTINUOUS   69

Paul and Joni climb off the bike. Nic storms out of the house to intercept them by the sidewalk.

> NIC
> Funny how someone *conveniently* forgot to tell me they were driving home on a motorcycle!

> JONI
> Mom...

57.

NIC
You know how many people I've seen come into the hospital paralyzed from motorcycle accidents?!

PAUL
I'm a very safe rider...

NIC
That is *so* not the point I'm making! Joni knows this is something I'd never allow.

JONI
Mom, I'm 18 years old! I won't even be living here in like next month!

NIC
Yeah, well, you're living here now!

JONI
Yeah, well why don't you get a jump on it and pretend like I'm not!

Joni storms off. Nic glowers at Paul.

NIC
She's never talked to me like that.

PAUL
(trying to soften it)
You know, Nic. If you eased up on the restrictions, maybe there'd be less tension...

NIC
(marinated in sarcasm)
Really? You think so, Paul? Is that how it works?

Jules walks up to intervene.

JULES
What's going on?

NIC
Oh, nothing. Paul's just giving me child-rearing lessons.

PAUL
I was just saying--

                    NIC
          Listen, when you've been a parent
          for 18 years, come talk to me!

                    PAUL
          I was just making an observation.

                    NIC
          Yeah, and I need your observations
          like I need a dick in my ass!

     Nic storms off. Jules follows. Paul watches, shell shocked.

70   OMITTED   70

71   INT. ALLGOOD HOUSE - JONI'S BEDROOM - LATER THAT NIGHT   71

     Nic knocks on the door. Get's no response.

                    NIC
          Joni?
               (silence)
          I was just upset. You know how I
          feel about motorcycles.

     Joni opens the door.

                    JONI
               (patronizing)
          I know how you feel about them.
          But I'm an adult now and you have
          to respect that. Goodnight.

     Joni closes the door on her.

72   OMITTED   72

73   INT. PAUL'S HOUSE - DAY   73

     From his house, Paul watches Jules working on her knees in
     the garden.

     CLOSE ON Jules' thong peaking out of her jeans. Luis walks
     across Paul's field of vision, interrupting his reverie.

74   INT. PAUL'S HOUSE - LATER   74

     Jules steps tentatively into Paul's house.

JULES
Paul?

Jules walks further into the house. She looks anxious. Paul opens his office door and sees Jules in the hall.

PAUL
Hey. What's up?

JULES
Look, I'm sorry about last night. I'm really embarrassed.

PAUL
Don't be. She's the one who wigged out.

JULES
I know, she's just going through a lot of stuff right now...

PAUL
Jules, it's okay. You don't have to defend her.

They stare at each other, unsure how to act.

JULES
And look, I just want you to know, about the other day, the kiss, that's not something I...do.

PAUL
Yeah, I sensed that.

She takes a step toward him, feverish.

JULES
I just wanted to clear the air.

They stare at each other. It's like watching two magnets.

PAUL
The air is clear.

Jules grabs Paul and starts smothering him with kisses.

It takes a second for Paul to get his bearings, but when he does, he starts kissing her back with equal fervor, pushing her up against the wall, wedging his hand between her legs.

JULES
Paul, I can't!

                    PAUL
          You don't want to?!

                    JULES
          No, I do! It's just...
               (urgent whisper)
          I have a guy outside!

Overcome with lust, Jules wraps her legs around his waist and
Paul walks her into...

75   HIS BEDROOM   75

Quick cuts of their awkward ravenous gropings. Somewhere
between slapstick and animal. He pulls her hair back hard.
She loves it. She pulls his hair back harder. He yelps.
She pulls down his underwear. Her eyes widen. It's been
decades since she's seen a hard cock in the flesh.

                    JULES
          Oh. Well. Hel-lo!

Cut to them fucking. It's gawky and passionate. Somewhere
in the middle of it, Jules starts laughing.

                    PAUL
          What?

                    JULES
          Nothing.

Paul flips her on her hands and knees and they go at it some
more.

She keeps laughing. Paul goes harder to make her stop. The
paces grows quicker. They're getting closer. And then...

                    LUIS (O.S.)
          Hello? Excuse me, Senora Allgood?!

They stop mid-thrust.

                    JULES
          You gotta be fucking kidding me!

She dislodges from Paul and starts dressing furiously.

76   INT./EXT. PAUL'S HOUSE - DAY   76

Jules runs out to meet Luis, waiting patiently at the door.

                    JULES
          What's up?

                    LUIS
          Where do you want the stones?

                    JULES
              (catching her breath)
          The stones? Over by the fence.

Luis stares at his employer. She looks totally disheveled.
Jules starts feeling her hair, smoothing it into shape.

                    JULES (CONT'D)
              (defensive)
          What? I was using the bathroom.
              (then)
          Do you need to use the bathroom?

Luis stares at her feet. She looks down. She's barefoot.

77   EXT. PUBLIC PARK - DAY   77

Paul and Laser shoot hoop. There's a tense-ness to their
patter. Laser takes the ball and steps to the top of the key
and shoots. Drains it.

                    LASER
          That's H.

                    PAUL
          I know.

Laser steps up to left side of the basket, calls his shot.

                    LASER
          Lay-up.

                    PAUL
          Hey, don't take it easy on me cause
          you're winning--

Laser does a trick behind the back lay-up. Nails it. Then
tosses the ball to Paul.

                    PAUL (CONT'D)
          Nobody likes a show-off.

                    LASER
          Hey, can I ask you a question?

PAUL
Oh god. Okay. Hit me.

LASER
When you die do you want to be buried or cremated?

PAUL
That's your question?

LASER
I want to be cremated.

PAUL
I think I'd rather be buried.

LASER
Why? That's just taking up more space in the earth.

PAUL
I don't know, something about the idea of being burned into this chalky powder and sprinkled--

LASER
What do you care? You won't even be conscious.

PAUL
That's true. I guess I just want to be in a place where people can visit me.

LASER
(growing animated)
But why?! You'll be dead! You won't even know they're there!

78 INT. WYSIWYG - RESTAURANT - NIGHT 78

Joni and Sasha are at a table eating dinner. Tanya has temporarily joined them. Sasha checks out Tanya's oversized African bead necklace. Joni watches Paul charm customers.

SASHA
God, I love your necklace! Where'd you get it?

TANYA
I don't know, some flea market--

SASHA
In Africa?

TANYA
No, more like Pasadena.

SASHA
Well, it's really awesome.

Paul saunters up to the table and stands behind Sasha. He mindlessly places his hand on Sasha's shoulder.

PAUL
Sorry guys, I need to steal Tanya back now.

Sasha clocks Paul's hand. She carefully and without looking back places her hand on top of his.

SASHA
That's okay, Paul.

TANYA
(getting up)
Well ladies, it was fun talking with you.

SASHA/JONI
You too.

Paul pulls his hand away from Sasha's and walks off with Tanya. Sasha turns to Joni.

SASHA
Okay, I'm sorry but your donor daddy is giving me the sex vibe.

JONI
No he's not. He wouldn't do that.

SASHA
Why not? He's not *my* dad.

JONI
God Sasha, that's totally gross! Not everybody wants to have sex with you, okay? Especially when you act like a slut.

SASHA
Fuck you.

> JONI
> Well it makes you seem insecure and desperate.
>
> SASHA
> I'm not insecure and desperate! I'm just a normal sexual person! And maybe you'd get that if you weren't so uptight!
>
> JONI
> Fuck you. I'm not uptight!

79   INT. RESTAURANT - NIGHT   79

Nic and Jules dine with their friends, JOEL and STELLA. Nic's drinking like a fish.

> STELLA
> Oh my god, these heirloom tomatoes are insane.
>
> JULES
> Joni brought some home from Paul's garden the other day. They were huge!

Nic tightens at the mention of Paul.

> JOEL
> So, the kids have been spending time with him?
>
> NIC
> Oh, yeah, they're spending all kinds of quality time together.
>
> STELLA
> (senses the sarcasm)
> Well, it's great they like him so much. You know, you hear these stories about kids meeting their donors and the guys end up being nothing like they were on paper.
>
> NIC
> No, everyone's getting along famously. Apparently Paul can do no wrong...

Nic grabs a passing waiter by the arm.

NIC (CONT'D)
Can we get another bottle of the
Seavey Cabernet?

Jules gives Nic a look. Joel and Stella feel the tension between them.

STELLA
Hey, have you guys tried those Açai
fruit packs?

JULES
No, but they're pushing them like
crack at Whole Foods.

STELLA
I know. Joel's addicted.

JOEL
What I do is I throw one in the
blender with some bananas, frozen
strawberries and hemp milk and I'll
tell you, it's sensational.

Nic slaps her forehead.

NIC
Oh, just fucking kill me...

Everyone stiffens. Jules is embarrassed.

JULES
Honey...

NIC
I'm sorry guys, but I just can't,
with the fucking hemp milk and the
organic farming and heirloom
tomatoes.
    (mocking-voice)
"Oh no, don't throw that in the
trash, no man, you gotta throw that
into the composting bin so the
fucking worms can shit all over it
and turn it into glorious multch
and we can all feel better about
ourselves." God! What a bunch of
bullshit!

Nic takes a big swallow from her glass. Jules windshield wipes Nic's forearm.

                    JULES
               (sotto)
          How about some green tea, honey...

     Nic slams her glass on the table. Explodes.

                    NIC
          You know what, Jules?! I like my
          wine! Okay? So fucking sue me!
          And fyi, red wine has a chemical
          called Resveratrol in it, which has
          been proven to significantly extend
          human lifespan!

                    JULES
          Yeah, if you drink a thousand
          bottles a day!

                    NIC
          Fuck you.

     Nic storms off. Jules turns to Joel and Stella, ashen.

                    JULES
          I'm sorry.

80   INT. RESTAURANT BAR - MINUTES LATER   80

     Jules walks over to the bar. Nic is sitting in the corner.

                    JULES
          What the hell is going on with you?

                    NIC
          This whole Paul thing is driving me
          crazy! I feel like he's taking
          over my family.

     Jules tries to bring it down. She yells in hushed tones.

                    JULES
          No. He's not!

                    NIC
               (nerves fraying)
          Okay! Okay. I'm sorry. I'm just
          exhausted...

                    JULES
          Maybe you need to take some time
          off and recharge.

                    NIC
               (self-pitying)
          Sure, and who's gonna pay for that?

Jules looks pissed off, and hurt.

                    NIC (CONT'D)
          Look, I'm sorry, I just feel like
          I'm carrying the whole load here.

                    JULES
          Because that's the way you like it!
          That's the way you keep control!

This is Jules' break-point.

                    NIC
          What are you talking about?

                    JULES
          Oh come on! You hated it when I
          worked! You wanted me at home,
          taking care of the kids. You
          wanted a wife!

                    NIC
          That is just not true!

                    JULES
          You didn't trust any of those
          nannies! And you sure as hell
          didn't back my career!

                    NIC
          What are you talking about? I just
          helped you start another business!

                    JULES
          Yeah, so you can feel better about
          yourself!

                    NIC
          No, so you can feel better about
          *your*self!

                    JULES
          Are you even attracted to me
          anymore?

The BARTENDER holds out the bottle of Cabernet.

                    BARTENDER
          Do you still want this?

                    NIC
          No. Just the check please.

81   JULES AND PAUL   81

      Fucking again in his bedroom. Jules writhes beneath him, her
      eyes closed. Paul seems to be in some kind of zone. He
      stares at her, enthralled.

                                                     CUT TO:

82   POST - COITUS   82

      Jules and Paul lie naked in the bed. Jules slithers around
      the covers, stoned on post-coital endorphins.

                    JULES
          God, I feel so drugular right now.
                (sitting up quickly)
          I really want a cigarette! Do you
          have any? I haven't had a
          cigarette since Laser was born. Do
          you smoke?

                    PAUL
          Sometimes. But I don't have any
          here. Want me to run to the store?

                    JULES
                (bouncing off the walls)
          Yeah. Wait, no. Don't. Sorry.

      Jules pops up on her knees, getting in his face.

                    JULES (CONT'D)
          Do you think I'm just like some sad-
          sack middle-aged lesbian?

                    PAUL
          God, that's it. I was trying to
          figure out how to describe you to
          my friends. Thank you.

      Jules punches his arm, mock hurt. They start rough-housing.
      Then kissing. Then the phone rings.

                    JULES
          You want to get that?

                    PAUL
          No. I want to get this...

Paul grabs a handful of Jules' ass. Jules throws her leg over Paul and climbs up for another round. Suddenly, Joni's voice echoes through the machine.

                    JONI (ON MACHINE)
        Hi Paul. It's Joni. I just wanted
        to apologize for my friend, Sasha.
        I was really embarrassed when she
        put her hand on your--

Paul grabs the receiver.

                    PAUL
        Hey, Joni. I'm here...

Jules visibly recoils.

                    PAUL (CONT'D)
        Listen, don't worry about your
        friend.

Jules pales. She mouths: "What are you doing?!" Paul gesticulates: "I'm sorry!"

                    PAUL (CONT'D)
        No. Honestly. I didn't even
        notice...

Jules throws on her clothes and starts to leave.

                    PAUL (CONT'D)
        Hey, Joni? Can you hold on a
        second?

Paul grabs Jules' wrist and mouths "wait!" Jules rips her arm free and walks out.

83   MOMENTS LATER - JULES   83

walks outside and is stunned to find Luis already back from Home Depot, sneezing and wiping his nose.

                    JULES
        Did you go to Home Depot?

                    LUIS
        Yeah. I just got back.

                    JULES
        That was fast!

                    LUIS
          Yeah, no lines.

His look of confusion trips off her paranoia. She's
convinced he knows everything.

                    JULES
          What's that look?

                    LUIS
          What look?

                    JULES
          The look you're giving me right
          now!

                    LUIS
          That's no look. That just my face.

                    JULES
          Look, I'm not gonna play this game
          with you! You need to keep your
          judgements to yourself!

                    LUIS
          Senora, I didn't give no looks!

                    JULES
          I don't ask you why you keep
          blowing your nose constantly! I
          mean, if you have a drug problem
          that's your business...

                    LUIS
          I don't have no drug problem!
          I have the allergies!

                    JULES
          Then why are you a gardener?!

Luis stares at Jules, innocent.

                    LUIS
          Cause I love the flowers.

                    JULES
          Look, this isn't gonna work. I'll
          pay you through the end of the day
          and then we're done.

Jules walks past a totally confused Luis.

84   INT. NIC AND JULES BEDROOM - NIGHT   84

Jules lies on her side. Nic shuffles to get to close to her. Jules moves away, still pissed at her. Nic realizes she needs to make amends.

85   INT. ALLGOOD HOUSE - KITCHEN - NEXT MORNING   85

The family sits in silence, having breakfast. Nic looks around the table, feeling like a pariah.

>   NIC
> Look, I know you've all been
> enjoying your time with Paul. And
> I know I haven't been as open to
> him as everyone else and this has
> caused some...friction...between
> us. But I'd like to try and change
> that...

Everyone keeps eating, uncommitted. "And...?"

>   NIC (CONT'D)
> So I was thinking. Maybe it would
> be nice if we all had dinner at his
> house sometime. That way, I could
> get to know him a little better,
> and I could see all the good work
> mom's been doing with his backyard.

Nic looks at Jules and smiles. Everyone nods. They recognize this is a big step for Nic.

86   OMITTED   86

87   EXT. PAUL'S HOUSE - BACKYARD - DAY   87

Paul walks out to check on Jules. She's sweating her ass off, shlepping stacks of heavy mulch across the yard.

>   PAUL
> How's it going?

>   JULES
> Okay...

                    PAUL
          Here, let me help.

Paul takes some of her load and together they transport the
sod to the other side of the yard. Neither know what to say.

Paul stares at her, waiting for her lead.

                    JULES
          We can't be doing this...

                    PAUL
          I know...

                    JULES
          I'm married...

                    PAUL
          ...and the kids...

                    JULES
          Yeah, and I love Nic.

                    PAUL
          I know...

They stare at each other and we cut to...

88   INT. PAUL'S BEDROOM - LATER   88

Paul and Jules lie in bed. Jules looks nauseated. Paul
offers her a pack of smokes.

                    PAUL
          I got you some cigarettes.

                    JULES
              (ignoring him)
          Jesus, what's wrong with me? I
          shouldn't have fired Luis like
          that. That was totally wrong...

                    PAUL
          Come on. Don't be so hard on
          yourself. Things get messy
          sometimes...

                    JULES
          That wasn't messy. That was fucked
          up. I'm totally fucked up...

                    PAUL
          I think I'm really falling for you.

                    JULES
          Paul, don't...

89   INT. PAUL'S BATHROOM - LATER   89

     Jules takes a shower, washing off the evidence. She looks
     nauseated by her lack of willpower.

90   INT. WYSIWYG - LATER   90

     Tanya walks over to Paul who's on his computer. She flops on
     the couch next to him. He doesn't look up.

                    TANYA
          Pretty good night. That table had
          like 5 bottles of wine.

                    PAUL
          Wow. Yeah. Good night.

                    TANYA
          Joni's pretty. She's got some of
          your genes.

                    PAUL
          I think she looks more like her mom
          actually. But thank you.

                    TANYA
          It's cute seeing you in dad mode.

                    PAUL
          Yeah?

                    TANYA
          Yeah.
               (lowering voice)
          It makes me want to fuck you.

                    PAUL
               (uncomfortable)
          Oh yeah?...

                    TANYA
          Yeah...

     Tanya moves imperceptibly closer.

                    TANYA (CONT'D)
          I've been missing our sleep-overs.

Paul finally stops what he's doing.

                    PAUL
          Yeah, it's been a while.

                    TANYA
          You want to meet up later?

Paul hesitates. He doesn't know how to say no.

                    PAUL
          Tanya, you're so sexy and
          beautiful, but I don't think we
          should do that anymore.

Tanya's face drops.

                    TANYA
          What happened?

                    PAUL
          You know, our thing is really fun
          and easy, but...I don't want to be
          50 and still "hanging out." You
          know? If I really want a family
          then I have to stop getting in
          these situations that don't go
          anywhere.

Paul just looks at her. Tanya gets it.

                    TANYA
                (welling up)
          Oh.

Paul knows enough to say nothing. Tanya gets up and walks off.

                    TANYA (CONT'D)
          Fuck you.

Paul sits there, feeling like an asshole.

91   EXT. ALLGOOD HOUSE - MAGIC HOUR   91

The family packs into the Volvo to head to Paul's.

92   INT. PAUL'S HOUSE - KITCHEN - MAGIC HOUR   92

Paul gets dinner ready with Joni and Laser as his sous-chefs. Both kids seem really jazzed to be cooking with him.

IN THE BACKYARD -EVENING

Jules tours Nic around the backyard, looking a little freaked out as she shows her the work she's been doing.

> JULES
> I'm gonna do some planting over there so it won't look so bare...

> NIC
> It looks great, honey. Very indigenous. I'm so proud of you.

Nic kisses Jules spontaneously. Jules looks nauseous again. They head back up the stairs, toward Paul's house.

> NIC (CONT'D)
> Hey, so how's that guy Luis working out?

> JULES
> Oh, I had to fire him.

> NIC
> (surprised)
> Really?!

> JULES
> Yeah, he had a drug problem.

> NIC
> Whoa. What kind of drugs?

> JULES
> Blow, I think...

93   INT. PAUL'S HOUSE - DINING ROOM - LATER   93

Nic flips through Paul's album collection, including Joni Mitchell's *Blue*.

94   INT. PAUL'S HOUSE - DINING ROOM - NIGHT   94

Everyone digs into the meal, enjoying themselves. Especially Nic, who's committed to redeeming herself.

PAUL
Hey Nic, I think you're gonna love this '98 Screaming Eagle.

NIC
You know what, I think I'm gonna stick with water tonight. But thank you so much.

The Allgoods look at Nic: this is a first.

NIC (CONT'D)
God, Paul, this steak is delicious. What's the seasoning?

PAUL
I just mist it with a little truffle oil.

Nic looks at Jules and smiles in full overcompensation mode.

NIC
What a good idea. We should try that. Right, honey?

JULES
(taken aback by Nic's cheerfulness)
Mmm-hmmm.

NIC
And it's done to perfection.

PAUL
So it's not too rare?

NIC
No, it's perfect. Juicy. Tender. Exactly what rare's supposed to be.

PAUL
Good. A lot of people in the restaurant order a steak rare and they freak out at the slightest sight of red.

NIC
Ugh, isn't that annoying? That happens to me all the time when I'm grilling.

                    PAUL
          Don't people know that rare means
          red?

                    NIC
          Right?! It means bloody!

                    PAUL
          Exactly! They should see what rare
          looks like in Argentina. The cow's
          practically still mooing.

Laser chuckles at Paul's joke, then reigns it in. Joni tries
to insert herself in the conversation.

                    JONI
          I really want to go to Argentina.
          Buenos Aires is supposed to be--

                    NIC
               (interrupting)
          ...So Paul, I was checking out your
          album collection over there. Quite
          the eclectic mix...

                    PAUL
          Thanks...

                    NIC
          You don't meet too many straight
          guys who love Joni Mitchell.

Joni glares at Nic: stop being such a Paul hog.

                    PAUL
          Oh yeah, you a Joni Mitchell fan?

                    NIC
               (smug)
          Not really. We just named our
          daughter after her.

                    PAUL
          Cool. Right on...

                    NIC
          What's your favorite Joni album?

                    PAUL
          I think I have to go with "Blue."

Nic raises her hand in a testify.

                    PAUL (CONT'D)
          Yeah? You too?

They high-five across the table.

                    NIC
          Oh God, I probably spent half of
          high school in my room crying to
          that album. That record kills me.

                    PAUL
          I know, it never lets up, you got
          "River," "California..."

                    NIC
          "A Case of You..."

                    PAUL
          "All I Want.."

                    NIC
          Mmm!!

Nic pulls her hands to her chest, shuts her eyes...and starts
to sing.

                    NIC (CONT'D)
          *I am on a lonely road and I am
          traveling traveling, traveling,
          traveling/Looking for something,
          what can it be/Oh I hate you some,
          I hate you some/I love you some Oh
          I love you/when I forget about
          me...*

Jules, Paul and the kids watch, open-mouthed as Nic soldiers
on, skipping ahead to another verse.

                    NIC (CONT'D)
          *I want to talk to you/I want to
          shampoo you/I want to renew you
          again and again/Applause, applause/
          Life is our cause/When I think of
          your kisses/My mind see-saws...*

Nic takes a breath. Just as Paul's about to say something,
Nic resumes her unfortunate solo.

                    NIC (CONT'D)
          *Do you see/do you see/do you see
          how you hu-urt me baby/so I hurt
          you too/then we both get/soo-ooo-
          ooo blue...*

Nic stops, eyes still closed. She's connected to a part of herself she rarely lets herself visit. The moment is punctured by her smart-ass 15-year-old son.

                    LASER
          Don't quit your day job, mom.

                    PAUL
          Hey. It's hard enough to open your
          heart in this world. Don't make it
          harder.

                    LASER
          You're right.
              (to Nic; contrite)
          I'm sorry, mom.

Nic looks at Paul. Stunned. Then looks at Jules and points to Paul.

                    NIC
          I like this guy.

Paul looks at Joni.

                    PAUL
          You didn't tell me you were named
          after Joni M.

                    JONI
          It's just so dorky. I don't really
          like to bring it up.

                    PAUL
          I think it's cool.

                    NIC
              (getting up)
          Hey Paul. Where's your bathroom?

                    PAUL
          Just around there.

On her way to the loo, Nic turns back to Paul.

                    NIC
          You know what? I think I will try
          some of that Screaming Eagle.

80.

95   INT. PAUL'S BATHROOM - CONTINUOUS   95

Nic washes her hands at the sink. Something catches her eye. She lifts Paul's hairbrush from the shelf in front of her and examines it. She reaches into the bristles and pulls out...

A few strands of long red hair.

Nic pales.

CUT TO

Nic on her knees in Paul's shower, pulling a clump of tell-tale red hair from the drain.

CUT TO

Nic skulks out of the bathroom. She looks out and b-lines for the bedroom.

CUT TO

Nic pulling pillows off Paul's bed. Her look tells us she's found hair here as well.

THEN WE CUT TO

Nic sitting back down at the table. She looks drained. Nobody notices. The sound drops out.

NIC'S POV:

Paul and Jules talking comfortably.

Joni and Laser chiming in, smiling, one big happy family.

REVERSE ONTO NIC:

Totally disconnected. Shell-shocked. She wants to scream but it feels like she's trapped in cement. Things slow way down...

96   OMITTED   96

97   INT. NIC AND JULES' BATHROOM - THAT NIGHT   97

Nic and Jules perform their nightly ablutions. Jules is sonic-caring her teeth.

JULES
(through the sonic buzz)
Well, you and Paul seemed to get on like gang-busters...

NIC
You're sleeping with him, aren't you.

JULES
(freaked)
What?

Nic turns to her, eyes red with anger.

NIC
Just be honest with me. Don't make me feel crazier than I feel right now!

JULES
Where is this coming from?!

NIC
I found your hair in his drain!

JULES
(scrambling)
What? I was working. I got dirty so I took a shower.

NIC
Oh yeah? You take a nap, too?

Jules pauses a second too long. The jig is up.

98 INT. NIC AND JULES' BEDROOM - MINUTES LATER 98

The truth has come out. Nic is so angry she's calm.

NIC
Are you in love with him?!

JULES
No!

NIC
What, are you straight now?!

JULES
No. It has nothing to do with that!
(MORE)

JULES (CONT'D)
(beat)
I've just felt so cut off from you lately...

NIC
Oh, right, so it's my fault!

JULES
No! Who said anything about fault? Just listen to me!

NIC
I'm listening! What?!

JULES
I just needed...

NIC
What? To be fucked?

JULES
No, appreciated!

NIC
It's always what I'm not doing for you, isn't it? Well here's what I don't *to* you. I don't work out my issues by fucking other people!

Nic starts heading for the door. Jules follows.

JULES
He's not just "other people!"

NIC
No, you had to go fuck our *sperm donor*! You couldn't have picked a more painful way to hurt me...

JULES
Where are you going?!

NIC
I need water! My mouth is dry!

Nic opens the door. There's Joni and Laser, looking devastated. They've been listening to the whole thing.

99   INT. ALLGOOD HOUSE - LIVING ROOM - DAWN   99

Jules wakes up looking crusty from a rough night on the couch. She looks like she hasn't slept at all.

100   INT. LASER'S ROOM - DAWN   100

Jules enters and walks over to her sleeping son. She gently nudges him awake.

> JULES
> Hey Laser. Honey?

Laser turns over, semi-conscious.

> LASER
> What?

She sits down on his bed.

> JULES
> Listen, I know you and Joni heard what's going on. I just want you to know that what happened with Paul and me is over. There's nothing going on now.

> LASER
> Okay.

> JULES
> I know you might need some time to process your feelings around this, but I just want you to know that I'm here for you if you want to talk about anything.
> (beat)
> Is there anything you want to talk about?

> LASER
> (leave my room)
> Not really.

> JULES
> (fighting the impulse to push it)
> Okay then. Go back to sleep.

Jules pats her son and leaves.

101   INT. JONI'S BEDROOM - DAWN   101

Jules enters and touches Joni's shoulder.

> JULES
> Joni?

                    JONI
          I don't want to talk to you.

                    JULES
          Can we just--

                    JONI
          I said I don't want to talk to
          you!!

                    JULES
          Okay. I'm sorry.

Jules slowly retreats to the door.

102   INT. ALLGOOD HOUSE - KITCHEN - MORNING   102

      Jules drinks coffee at the table. Nic walks in, dressed for
      work. Jules looks at her, wanting to "process." But Nic
      isn't in the mood. She grabs a banana from a bowl and walks
      out. Jules feels like a leper.

103   OMITTED.   103

104   INT. SASHA'S ROOM - AFTERNOON   104

      We can tell Joni's been crying and downloading the whole
      thing to Sasha.

                    SASHA
          How's Nic doing?

                    JONI
          She's a wreck. I've never seen her
          like this before.

      Joni's cell rings. She gets off the bed, looks at the phone.
      It's a picture of Paul.

                    SASHA
          Is it him...?

      Joni nods gravely, answers.

                    JONI
               (cold)
          Hello.

105   EXT. PAUL'S FARM - AFTERNOON   105

Paul's walking through rows of swiss chard, cell phone to his ear.

Conversation Intercut.

                    PAUL
          Hey Joni, how you doing?

                    JONI
          You're such a phony.

Beat.

                    PAUL
          Excuse me?

                    JONI
          You act like you're so groovy and
          together but you're not. You're a
          shitty person!

                    PAUL
          What happened?

                    JONI
          With my mom?!

                    PAUL
          Listen, can I just come and talk
          with you--

                    JONI
          What's wrong with you?!

                    PAUL
          Joni...

                    JONI
          Don't call me anymore.

Joni hangs up and start crying. Sasha hugs her.

106   EXT. PAUL'S FARM - CONTINUOUS   106

Sweaty, nauseous with remorse, Paul turns around to find fetching young Brooke, waiting for him with a wicker basket of huge cucumbers.

                    BROOKE
          Hey Paul, look at these cukes...

Paul holds up his hand at her. This girl symbolizes every bad choice he's ever made.

He gives her the universal, "Leave Me Alone" gesture. Brooke looks embarrassed.

107 EXT. ALLGOOD HOUSE - BACKYARD - AFTERNOON   107

Jules sits on a lawn chair smoking a cigarette. Her cell rings. She answers.

108 EXT. STREET - AFTERNOON   108

Paul walks down the street, wigging out.

                    PAUL
          Hey, it's me. I just talked to
          Joni.

Conversation intercut.

                    JULES
          Oh my god, I'm so sorry. I should
          have called you.

Jules sucks a big, anxious drag off a cigarette.

                    PAUL
          What happened?

                    JULES
          Nic saw my hair in your bathroom.

                    PAUL
          The other night.

                    JULES
          Yeah.

                    PAUL
          Fuck...

                    JULES
          Yeah.

Beat.

                    PAUL
          Listen, it's all out in the open
          now. Let's make this happen.

                    JULES
          Paul...

                    PAUL
          No, I'm serious. Fuck it. Let's get
          the kids together and do this
          thing.

                    JULES
          Paul, come on...

                    PAUL
          No! I'm sick of this life. I want
          a family. I'm ready--

                    JULES
               (eye rolling)
          Jesus, Paul! I'm gay!

Jules tosses the phone away from her.

109   EXT. HOUSE PARTY - BACKYARD - NIGHT   109

Joni and Sasha stand at the makeshift "bar". Joni's downs
several Tequila shots quickly.

                    SASHA
          Slow down, tiger.

Across the room, Joni spots Jai chatting with a WAIFY GIRL in
a sundress.

Joni drops one more Tequila shot and walks up to Jai and
Waify girl, interrupting them.

                    JONI
          I like the scruff. It's sexy.

Waify girl juts out her hip territorially.

                    WAIFY GIRL
          Uh, 'scuuuse me...

                    JONI
          You're excused.
               (then back to Jai)
          Hey, can I talk to you?

Joni leads Jai to a private corner.

She leans in and kisses Jai. And Jai actually returns the kiss. And it's completely sweet and intimate.

But then the kiss starts to morph as Joni's energy turns manic, intense, less romantic than emotionally needy. We see Jai start to pull away. But Joni keeps holding him, wanting more. Finally, Jai breaks off the kiss.

                    JAI
          Joni...Joni...

                    JONI
          What?

Joni looks pained, embarrassed. Jai keeps holding her hands.

                    JAI
          Are you okay?

                    JONI
          Yeah, I'm fine...

Joni pulls free and escapes, leaving a confused Jai in her wake.

110   INT. NIC AND JULES BEDROOM - NIGHT   110

Jules walks in to find Nic, awake, in bed.

                    JULES
          Just getting another pillow. The
          couch is kind of saggy.

                    NIC
          Is your back okay?

Jules perks up: is this an invitation to share the bed again?

                    JULES
          It's a little ache-y.

                    NIC
          You should take some Advil.

Guess not.

Suddenly they hear bumping and loud footsteps downstairs.

111   INT. ALLGOOD HOUSE - LIVING ROOM - NIGHT   111

Jules walks downstairs to find Joni stumbling toward her bedroom.

                    JULES
          Hey. How was the party?

Joni tries to avert her mom's questioning gaze.

                    JONI
          Fine.

                    JULES
          How big was it?

                    JONI
          I don't know. Medium...ish...

Jules takes in the glassy look in her daughter's eyes.

                    JULES
          Are you drunk?

                    JONI
          No.

Nic enters from the stairs, having caught the last piece.

                    NIC
          I hope you had a designated driver.

                    JONI
          Why? I'm not drunk.

                    NIC
          Well, you seem drunk to me.

                    JONI
          Yeah, well, you should know.

                    NIC
              (furious; incredulous)
          What did you just say to me?!

                    JONI
          I'm going to bed.

Joni starts to leave. Nic grabs her.

                    NIC
          No, you're not! I'm not done
          talking to you!

Laser opens his door and watches the scene progress.

> JONI
> What do you want from me?! I did everything you wanted! I got all A's! I got in everywhere I applied! Now you can show everybody what a perfect family you have!

> JULES
> Don't talk to your mom like that!

Joni spins to face Jules.

> JONI
> You're really gonna tell *me* how to act? Now?!

> JULES
> Hey, I'm still your mother.

> JONI
> Whatever...

Jules reaches out and Joni backs away, sickened.

> JONI (CONT'D)
> Don't touch me!

Joni heads for her room.

> JONI (CONT'D)
> I'm so sick of both of you!

112 EXT. ALLGOOD HOUSE - DAWN - MOS   112

The sun rises on this formerly happy home.

113 INT. ALLGOOD LIVING ROOM - MORNING   113

Jules wakes up on the couch. Sits up. Rubs her aching back.

114 INT. ALLGOOD HOUSE - JONI'S BEDROOM - DAY   114

Joni packs for college. The room is littered with half-filled packing boxes. She picks up a pile of clothes from the corner and sees the farmer's hat Paul gave her. She puts it aside, not sure what to do with it.

115   EXT. PAUL'S BACKYARD - DAY   115

Paul looks around his newly landscaped yard. It looks more abandoned than revived.

116   INT. ALLGOOD HOUSE - NIGHT   116

The family has their last supper - before Joni leaves.

                    NIC
          Did you pack that lamp I gave you?

                    JONI
          Yeah.

                    NIC
          Well, we can always get stuff up
          there, too, if you need it, I mean
          if the room's dark or you need
          extra bedding...

                    JONI
          I'm not going to Siberia, mom.

Jules looks at the family unit, misty.

                    JULES
          I can't believe this is our last
          dinner together.

                    LASER
          Oh God, are you gonna cry?

Jules looks at her son, fed up.

                    JULES
          I wish you *were* gay. You'd be so
          much more sensitive.

The doorbell rings.

                    JONI
          It's probably Sasha. I'll get it.

Joni runs to the door. Opens it. It's not Sasha. It's Paul.

                    JONI (CONT'D)
              (shocked)
          What are you doing here?

                    PAUL
          I needed to talk to you before you
          left.

                    JONI
          There's nothing to talk about.

                    PAUL
          I just want to apologize again for
          what happened. I can't tell you
          how much I regret it.

117   EXT. ALLGOOD HOUSE - SAME   117

Joni walks out for privacy, closes the door behind her.

                    JONI
          So like, everything that happened
          between us. What was that? Was
          that just bullshit?!

                    PAUL
          No, it wasn't bullshit at all. I
          know I don't seem credible right
          now but I really care about you...

Paul struggles to keep his emotions in check.

                    PAUL (CONT'D)
          ...and I just hope someday we'll be
          able to see each other again. Do
          you think that could maybe happen?

                    JONI
          I don't know...

Joni looks down welling up.

                    JONI (CONT'D)
          I just wish you could've been...

                    PAUL
          What?

Joni chokes back tears.

                    JONI
          Better...

Paul and Joni look up at each other when the door suddenly
flings open. Nic is there, fuming.

                    NIC
          You've got some balls, mister!

                    PAUL
          Nic, hold on...

Nic walks toward he and Joni. Joni ducks back inside.

                    NIC
          No, you hold on! Let me tell you
          something, you really hurt my kids!

                    PAUL
          Well, they're kinda my...

                    NIC
              (cutting him off)
          No! They're not. This is *not* your
          family. This is *my* family! You're
          just a fucking interloper...

Jules joins Nic, concerned things are getting out of hand.

                    PAUL
          I didn't mean to hurt anyone...

Paul and Jules share a look as Nic deals the *coup de grace*.

                    NIC
          If you want a family so much, go
          out and make one of your own!

Nic heads back inside and slams the door behind her.

Paul stand alone, spinning. After a moment he spontaneously looks back into the house. Laser is staring at him through the window. Their eyes lock and Paul give Laser a contrite smile. That's the final straw for Laser. He grabs his plate and walks out of view.

Reeling, Paul heads for his motorcycle. He gets on the bike, helmet in hand. Turns on the ignition. He picks up the helmet and pauses, shaking in the hell of his own making. Losing it, he hurls the helmet at the motorcycle.

118   INT. ALLGOOD HOUSE - TV ROOM - THAT NIGHT   118

Laser, Joni and Nic watch "Locked Up Abroad" Jules walks in front of them, picks up the remote and turns off the TV.

                    JULES
          I need to say something.

Everyone sits up. Jules acts stoic but she's wrecked.

> JULES (CONT'D)
> Look, it's no big secret your mom and are in hell right now. Bottom line...marriage is hard...really fucking hard. Just two people, slogging through the shit, year after year, getting older, changing. It's a fucking marathon, okay?!

Everyone is silenced by the outpouring. Jules soldiers on.

> JULES (CONT'D)
> So sometimes you're together so long, you just stop seeing the other person. You just see weird projections of your own junk. And instead of talking to each other, you go off the rails, and act grubby and make stupid choices. Which is what I did. And I feel sick about it because I love you guys and I love your mom and that's the truth. Sometimes you hurt the ones you love the most. I don't know why. Maybe if I read more Russian novels I would...

Nic looks down, overwhelmed by it all.

> JULES (CONT'D)
> Anyway, I just wanted to say how sorry I am about what I did and that I hope you'll forgive me eventually.
> (awkward)
> Thank you.

And, without further ado, Jules hands the remote back to Laser and departs the field. Everyone's silenced by Jules' rambling apologia, especially Nic.

119   OMITTED.   119

120   INT. JONI'S ROOM - MORNING   120

Joni wakes up. She looks around her room. There's nothing on the walls. The floor is covered with boxes taped and labeled. It's time to go.

95.

121	EXT. ALLGOOD HOUSE - DRIVEWAY - DAY	121

Nic and Jules stuff the last of Joni's things in the back of their station wagon. Laser and Joni bring the last of the boxes out of the house.

122	INT. VOLVO STATION WAGON - DAY	122

The Allgoods are on the road, heading to college.

123	OMITTED.	123

124	EXT. COLLEGE CAMPUS - DAY - ESTABLISHING	124

The station wagon passes through the campus.

125	INT. STATION WAGON - DAY	125

As they drive past buildings and dorms, Joni sees STUDENTS swarming the campus. She takes it all in, nervous, excited. Nic and Jules steal looks back at Joni, feeling her nervousness, wishing they could take it away.

126	EXT. STREET - DAY	126

The Allgoods pull up to the curb, get out. Laser piles Joni's boxes on his skateboard.

127	EXT. FRONT OF DORM - DAY	127

Laser dollies Joni's boxes though the corridor and while Joni and the moms follow behind.

INT. DORM ROOM - MOMENTS LATER

Nic and Jules follow Joni to the door. They all jam up at the threshold.

                    JONI
          Guys, it's okay. I got it.

Nic and Jules get the hint. They move back and Joni enters the room alone. Nic and Jules quietly turn and leave.

128 INT. JONI'S DORM ROOM - BEDROOM - LATER   128

Joni stands among her bags and boxes looking around. She goes into her suitcase and pulls out her linens. She starts making her bed but suddenly stops mid way. She stares out toward the hallway.

Finally she moves to the doorway and looks out. She realizes her family isn't there.

129 EXT. DORM BUILDING - DAY   129

Joni exits, looking around to find her family. The station wagon is gone. She looks panicked. Her pace quickens as she makes her way down a hill toward the road.

Finally Joni sees the Volvo heading towards her.

The car pulls over to the curb and everyone gets out. Joni looks vulnerable. She tries to cover it.

                    JONI
          Where'd you go?!

                    NIC
          We had to move the car.

                    JONI
          I thought you left.

                    JULES
          We wouldn't leave without saying
          goodbye.

                    NIC
          Give us *some* credit.

And suddenly, everyone realizes...this is it. It's time to say goodbye. First Laser comes up and hugs Joni.

                    LASER
          It's gonna be weird not having you
          at home.

                    JONI
          Sorry to leave you alone with them.

                    LASER
          It's okay. I can handle it.

Laser backs up. Then the moms both come up and hug Joni, tears streaming down their faces.

                    JONI
          Guys, come on...
               (beat)
          Look, I'll talk to you soon.

Joni tries to detach from the hug. But her moms won't let
go. They keep holding her and crying.

Slowly, their tears begin to break Joni down.

Trapped in their loving embrace, Joni's feelings rise up,
unbidden, overpowering her. She starts crying.

The moms hold her tighter, which makes her cry even harder.

Soon she's sobbing in her mothers' arms, as all the pressure,
resentment and anger she's felt starts seeping out of her.

Nic and Jules feel their daughter letting go. They hold her
tight to comfort her.

They keep holding her until a calm sets in.

The hug breaks apart. Nic pushes the hair from Joni's face.
Joni gives her moms one last smile.

Laser, Jules and Nic get back in the car. Joni stands
watching as they drive off and her new life begins.

130   INT. STATION WAGON - DAY   130

The family drives home. Jules is at the wheel. Nic's in the
passenger seat, eyes red and puffy. Laser's in the back.

No one speaks, everyone's lost in their own worlds. Finally
Laser breaks the spell.

                    LASER
          I don't think you guys should break
          up.

A long beat.

                    NIC
          No? Why's that?

                    LASER
          I think you're too old.

Both Nic and Jules crack smiles. Their son's rudeness is
unsurpassed. But then his words have an unexpected gravity.

                    NIC
          Thanks, Laser.

Jules, disarmed and slightly smiling, reaches over and puts
her hand on Nic's leg. She gives it a gentle squeeze and
doesn't let go. Nic looks over to Jules, finally disarmed.

Nic reaches for Jules' hand and holds it tight. Nic and
Jules look at each other, and then away.

Laser watches his moms holding hands from the back seat.
Their small gesture is what he needed. He smiles to himself,
grateful for a sign.

FADE OUT

THE END

STILLS

Julianne Moore as Jules

Annette Bening as Nic

Mia Wasikowska as Joni and Josh Hutcherson as Laser

Mark Ruffalo as Paul

Nic and Jules at home watching television, beckoning to Laser.

Nic welcoming Paul on his first visit to the house.

Nic and Jules sizing up Paul.

Paul and Laser hanging out together.

Nic consoling Jules.

Laser and the moms saying goodbye to Joni at her college.

CAST AND CREW CREDITS

A FOCUS FEATURES and GILBERT FILMS presentation in association with SAINT AIRE PRODUCTIONS, ARTIST INTERNATIONAL, and 10TH HOLE PRODUCTIONS of an ANTIDOTE FILMS, MANDALAY VISION, and GILBERT Films production.
A Film by LISA CHOLODENKO

ANNETTE BENING   JULIANNE MOORE   MARK RUFFALO

THE KIDS ARE ALL RIGHT

MIA WASIKOWSKA and JOSH HUTCHERSON

Casting by
LAURA ROSENTHAL

Music Supervisor
LIZA RICHARDSON

Music by
CARTER BURWELL

Editor
JEFFREY M. WERNER

Costumes Designer
MARY CLAIRE HANNAN

Production Designer
JULIE BERGHOFF

Director of Photography
IGOR JADUE-LILLO

Produced by
GARY GILBERT
JEFFREY LEVY-HINTE
CELINE RATTRAY
JORDAN HOROWITZ
DANIELA TAPLIN LUNDBERG
PHILIPPE HELLMANN

Written by
LISA CHOLODENKO &
STUART BLUMBERG

Directed by
LISA CHOLODENKO

A Focus Features Release

CAST

Jules . . . . JULIANNE MOORE
Nic . . . . ANNETTE BENING
Paul . . . . MARK RUFFALO
Joni . . . . MIA WASIKOWSKA
Laser . . . . JOSH HUTCHERSON
Tanya . . . . YAYA DaCOSTA
Jai . . . . KUNAL SHARMA
Clay . . . . EDDIE HASSELL
Sasha . . . . ZOSIA MAMET
Luis . . . . JOAQUIN GARRIDO
Brooke . . . . . REBECCA LAWRENCE
Stella . . . . LISA EISNER
Joel . . . . ERIC EISNER
Waify Girl . . . . . . SASHA SPIELBERG
Clay's Dad . . . . . JAMES MacDONALD
Bartender . . . . MARGO VICTOR

Stunt Coordinator. . . . . MARK NORBY
Stunts. . . . . SEAN GRAHAM
. . . . CASSIDY HICE
. . . . WILLIAM SPENCER
Stunt Safety/Rigger
. . . . DARRELL CRAIG DAVIS

CREW

Directed by . . . . LISA CHOLODENKO
Written by . . . . . LISA CHOLODENKO
                    & STUART BLUMBERG
Produced by . . . . GARY GILBERT
JEFFREY LEVY-HINTE
CELINE RATTRAY
JORDAN HOROWITZ
DANIELA TAPLIN LUNDBERG
PHILIPPE HELLMANN
Executive Producers . . STEVEN SAXTON
RON STEIN
RIVA MARKER
ANNE O'SHEA
CHRISTY CASHMAN
ANDREW SAWYER
NEIL KATZ
J. TODD HARRIS
Co-Producers. . . . BERGEN SWANSON
LAURA ROSENTHAL
CHARLES E. BUSH, JR.
TODD LABAROWSKI
JOEL NEWTON
CAMILLE MOREAU
Director of Photography
. . . . IGOR JADUE-LILLO
Production Designer . . JULIE BERGHOFF

Editor. . . . . . JEFFREY M. WERNER
Music by. . . . . . CARTER BURWELL
Music Supervisor. . LIZA RICHARDSON
Costume Designer
. . . . MARY CLAIRE HANNAN
Casting by . . . . LAURA ROSENTHAL
Los Angeles Casting by . LIZ DEAN, C.S.A.

Unit Production Manager
. . . . BERGEN SWANSON
First Assistant Director . . . . . JESSE NYE
Second Assistant Director
. . . . . JASMINE MARIE ALHAMBRA
Sound Design and Supervision
. . . . FRANK GAETA
and ELMO WEBER
Production Supervisor
. . . . TRACEY LANDON
Set Decorator . . . . DAVID COOK
Script Supervisor . . . . REBECCA
ROBERTSON-SZWAJA
Production Coordinator . . MARK ASARO
"A" 1st Assistant Camera/"B" Camera
Operator. . . . . . . MARK FIGUEROA
"A" 2nd Assistant Camera
. . . . GASTON RICHMOND
"B" 1st Assistant Camera
. . . . LEONCIO PROVOSTE
"B" 2nd Assistant Camera . . ALEX SCOTT
Loader . . . . AARON TICHENOR
Costume Supervisor
. . . . JACQUELINE ARONSON
Set Costumer . . . LISA MARIE HARRIS
Costumer . . . KATHRYN L. BUCHER
Additional Costumers . . RIKI SABUSAWA
SIERRA BAY ROBINSON
Head Ager/Dyer. . . . SHARON FAUVEL
Co-Make-up Department Heads
. . . . ELAINE OFFERS
VALLI O'REILLY
Make-up Artist . . . . RONNIE SPECTER
Hair Department Head
. . . . CYDNEY CORNELL
Key Hair Stylists . . . . . . CARL BAILEY
DANIEL CURET
Hair Stylist. . . . JASON ORION GREEN
Gaffer. . . . . DAYTON NIETERT
Best Boy Electric . . . . JESSE RUSHTON
Electricians . . CHRISTOPHER BERNAL
DAVID BOUZA
RICK CRONN
ERIK A. ERICHSEN
JOHN JOLEAUD
JASON P. SALINAS
MIGUEL SANCHEZ
Rigging Gaffer . . . . BILL GREENBERG
Rigging Electricians. . CARSON E. MAYNE
DOUG I. SOTO
Balloon Technician . . . . . NEIL YOUNG
Key Grip. . . . . GREG KARAMOV
Best Boy Grip . . . DEMETRIE COOLEY
Dolly Grip. . . . . . SETH GREENWALD
Grips . . . . . . TIGRAN AGHASARYAN
EDWARD V. BAUMAN
RICKY DIAZ
OSCAR GARCIA
JORDAN GARRETSON
JEFFREY B. GREGG
VADIM FRUMIN LANDAU
JULIAN S. LOPEZ
JOSE A. SANTIAGO
ADAM SHEEDY
FRED TROESKEN
Rigging Key Grip . . . TED S. KENNEDY
Rigging Best Boy Grip
. . . . MICHAEL DiGIOVANNI
Rigging Grips. . . . . ALEX GAGE
MICHAEL E. PACHECO
CHRIS B. ROUNTREE
Sound Mixer . . JOSE ANTONIO GARCIA
Boom Operator
. . . . . . JONATHAN LEE-GER FUH
Utility Sound . . . . . ERIC A. BAUTISTA
Special Effects Technician . . NEIL SMITH
Propmaster. . . . . JEFFREY M. O'BRIEN
Assistant Propmaster. . . KAREN HOLLEY
Assistant Props . . . . . GREG HOLLEY
CRAIG GLENN
Food Stylist . . . . . . APRIL FALZONE
Art Director. . JAMES PEARSE CONNELLY
Art Department Coordinator
. . . . CINDY PETERS
Standby Painter. . . . . KATIA KAPLUN
Painter . . . LISA MATSUURA WALKER
Leadman . . . . . JAMES A. COSTELLO
On-Set Dresser . . . . . JOSH ELLIOTT
Set Dressers. . . LEONARDO COLEMAN
COLMAN COSTELLO
CHRISTOPHER W.J. DINAN
MORGAN GILLIO
STEVE KELLEY JR.
MARTIN CARRASCO LEON
GREG MANKE
JOHN STONE
Greensperson . . . . . CHRISTINE EYER
Assistant Production Coordinator
. . . . COURTNEY LaBREE
Production Accountant . . ROBERT CABLE

1st Assistant Accountant
. . . . MARGARET MARTINEZ
Payroll Accountants . . ILANA McALLISTER
DAN HEMPHILL
Location Manager . . . . . NED SHAPIRO
Key Assistant Location Manager
. . . . CHARLES FAGIN
Assistant Location Managers
. . . . SHAWN HUESTON
JEFF KORSON
Location Scout . . MARIE PAULE GOISLARD
EPK . . . . MARK SHOCKLEY
Still Photographer . . SUZANNE TENNER
2nd 2nd Assistant Director . . EMILY HOGAN
Key Production Assistant . . JACKSON ROWE
Set Production Assistants . . LESLIE MERLIN
TYLER BEEM
SAM K. NAINOA III
MEGAN SCHMIDT
ROBERT MORRIS
WILLIAM BATSEL
CAROLINE FIFE
MEREDITH
ANNE GREENBERG
ALEX O'FLINN
HENRIK PELLIER
DIANA VAN LEEUWEN
NICOLAS ZAPATA
Office Production Assistants . . LILI ROMERO
DONALD CHAMBERS
Casting Associates . . . . MARIBETH FOX
ERIC SOULIERE, C.S.A.
Extras Casting . . . . . CHRIS BUSTARD
Cast/Producer's Assistant . . . TIFFANY LO
Assistant to Ms. Moore
. . . . . CAROLINE T. APPLEGARTH
Assistant to Mr. Ruffalo
. . . . WEDNESDAY STANDLEY
Assistant to Ms. Cholodenko
. . . . NATHANIEL STUTZ
Assistant to Mr. Gilbert
. . . . SHAUNA BOGETZ
Assistant to Mr. Levy-Hinte . . PAUL T. LIST
Executive in Charge of Production,
Mandalay Vision . . . . . NIC MARSHALL
Development Executive, Mandalay Vision
. . . . JENNY HALPER
Video Playback Coordinator
. . . . LUCAS SOLOMON
Video Technician . . . . VERNON EVANS
Transportation Coordinator . GENO HART
Transportation Captains
. . . . ADAM PINKSTAFF
HARDY OPHULS

Transportation Co-Captain
. . . . JOHN PELLEGRINO
Picture Vehicle Captain
. . . . MARTIN OSBOURNE
Drivers . . . . LUKE H. ATKINE
TONY BARATTINI
MICHAEL R. BELT
JODY BINGENHEIMER
ANGEL DE SANTI
AUDREY FITZGERALD
WAYNE FLOWERS
CRHIS HAYNES
KIRK HUSTON
CARLOS M. SERRANO
STEVE WEIBLE
DAVE WILSON
Head Chef . . . . JAMIE KEMP
Chef/Driver . . SANTOS P. RODRIGUEZ
Cooks . . . . BRIAN NAILING
ANDRES M. HERNANDEZ
Craft Service . . . . . GARY WOLDMAN
Set Medics . . . . DANIEL SHINE
TONY PENIDO
Studio Teachers . . HEATHER FIELDING
JACK STERN
Stand-In for Ms. Moore . . CELIA HEMKEN
Stand-In for Ms. Bening & Ms. Wasikowska
. . . . TONI KALLEN
Stand-In for Mr. Ruffalo . . . GABE DELL
Interns . . . . . . ALEXANDRA DUNN
LENNON FICALORA
BIANCA POLETTI
RACHEL ROSALES

Post-Production

Post-Production Supervisor
. . . . JAMES DEBBS
Additional Editor
. . . . NANCY RICHARDSON, A.C.E.
First Assistant Editor . . . . BOB DRWILA
Audio Post Services provided by
. . . . SOUND FOR FILM
Re-recording Mixers . . . ELMO WEBER
FRANK GAETA
PATRICK GIURAUDI
Sound Editor . . . . JOE IEMOLA
Foley Recordist . . . . . DARRIN MANN
Foley Artists . . . CATHERINE HARPER
CHRIS MORIANNA
Music Editor . . . . JENNY BARAK
Music composed, arranged and conducted by
. . . . CARTER BURWELL
Score Recording Engineer
. . . . MICHAEL FARROW
Assistant Engineer . . . . . BRYAN SMITH

Composer's Assistant . . . DEAN PARKER
Score recorded at . . . . CLINTON RECORDING STUDIO, NEW YORK
Score mixed at . . . THE BODY STUDIO, NEW YORK

Musicians

Guitar. . . . . MARC RIBOT
Bass. . . . . JOHN PATTITUCCI
Keyboards . . . . . . CARTER BURWELL

Dolby Stereo Consultant. . TREVOR WARD
Main Title Design . . . ANDY GOLDMAN
Digital Visual Effects . . . . + SCALE
Lead Visual Effects Compositor. . TODD SINES
Visual Effects Compositors
. . . . CHARLOTTA FORSSMAN
SUNG KYU KOO
+ SCALE Executive Producer
. . . . MARCUS LANSDELL
Dailies Laboratory . . . . TECHNICOLOR NORTH HOLLYWOOD
Dailies Colorist . . . . . MARC WIELAGE
Dailies Project Manager. . DEANNA O'NEIL
Post Services provided by . . TECHNICOLOR DIGITAL INTERMEDIATES
Digital Film Colorist . . . JASON FABBRO
Digital Intermediate Producer. . ESTHER LEE
Digital Intermediate Editor
. . . . MARK SAHAGUN
Digital Color Assistant . . DAN WILLIAMS
Imaging Technicians. . . . FLOYD BURKS
Digital Restoration . . . . BRAD SUTTON
WILSON TANG
Data Technicians . . . . . . DON HENRY
TIM HEUGELE
Imaging R&D . . . . JOSHUA PINES
Engineering . . . . . . MARK HUBBARD
Technicolor Executive . . . DIANE UPSON
Technicolor Key Account Manager
. . . . DAN WESSELMAN
Technicolor Customer Service Representative
. . . . DON COWAN
Manager Sound Services – Video Film Audio Forensics . . . . . . MICAH LITTLETON
Financing and Distribution Advisory Services
. . . . CINETIC MEDIA
Financing provided by
. . . . CITY NATIONAL BANK, RICHARD McCUNE and ERIK PIECUCI
Production Insurance provided by
. . . . KATHY ENGLAND AT TAYLOR & TAYLOR, LTD.

Songs

"COUSINS"
Written by Ezra Koenig, Rostam Batmanglij, Chris Baio and Chris Tomson
Performed by Vampire Weekend
Courtesy of XL Recordings Ltd.
By arrangement with The Beggars Group

"OUT IN THE WOODS"
Written and performed by Leon Russell
Courtesy of Capitol Records
Under license from EMI Film & TV Music

"TAILGATING"
Written by Thomas Hirschmann, Steven Stern and Stuart Hart
Performed by Tom Hirschmann
By arrangement with Selectracks

"SUNDOWN SYNDROME"
Written by Kevin Parker
Performed by Tame Impala
Courtesy of Universal Music Australia Pty. Ltd. Under license from Universal Music Enterprises
By arrangement with Bank Robber Music

"PANIC IN DETROIT"
Written by David Bowie
Performed by David Bowie
Courtesy of RZO Music

"WIN"
Written by David Bowie
Performed by David Bowie
Courtesy of RZO Music

"MILK MAN"
Written by Greg Saunier, Satomi Matsuzaki, Chris Cohen and John Dieterich
Performed by Deerhoof
Courtesy of Kill Rock Stars
By arrangement with Terrorbird Media

"A MATAR EN LA DISCO"
Written by Heath Brennan
Performed by Trespeso
Courtesy of True Music, LLC

"SLIPPIN"
Written by Robert Braun and Coco Karshøj
Performed by Quadron
Courtesy of Plug Research Records
By arrangement with Visions From The Roof

"RED HANDED"
Written by Thomas Hirschmann,
Steven Stern and Saul Hart
Performed by Tom Hirschmann
By arrangement with Selectracks

"BLACK COUNTRY ROCK"
Written by David Bowie
Performed by David Bowie
Courtesy of RZO Music

"BLUE CASH"
Written by Greg Saunier,
Satomi Matsuzaki, Chris Cohen
and John Dieterich
Performed by Deerhoof
Courtesy of Kill Rock Stars
By arrangement with Terrorbird Media

"THE NEW WORLD"
Written by John Doe and Exene Cervenka
Performed by X
Courtesy of Elektra Entertainment
By arrangement with WMG Film and TV Licensing

"SAME HIGH"
Written by
Camila "Grey" Gutierrez
and Leisha Hailey
Performed by Uh Huh Her
By arrangement with
Nettwerk Music Group

"WHEN I GROW UP (D LISSVIK REMIX)"
Written by Karin Dreijer-Andersson
Performed by Fever Ray
Courtesy of Rabid Records
under exclusive license to Mute
Under license from EMI Film & TV Music

"BLUES ALLEY"
Written by Gerard Young and Yukimi Nagano
Performed by Ge-ology featuring Yukimi Nagano
Courtesy of Mineral Werks
By arrangement with Bug

"GALATEA'S GUITAR"
Written and performed by
Gabor Szabo
Courtesy of
Lilac Drive Records

"FORTUNE"
Written by Hakan Wirestrand, Erik Bodin,
Fredrik Kallgren-Wallin and Yukimi Nagano
Performed by Little Dragon
Courtesy of Peacefrog

"GOOD LOVIN' "
Written by Willie Clark,
Johnny Pearsall and Clarence Reid
Performed by Betty Wright
Courtesy of The Numero Group
By arrangement with Bank Robber Music

"ALL I WANT"
Written by Joni Mitchell

"KNIFE"
Written by Edward Droste, Daniel Rossen,
Christopher Bear and Christopher Taylor
Performed by CSS
Courtesy of Sub Pop Records

"THE YOUTH"
Written by Andrew VanWyngarden
and Benjamin Goldwasser
Performed by MGMT
Courtesy of Columbia Records
By arrangement with Sony Music Licensing

Scrabble used by permission of Mattel, Inc./
Scrabble appears courtesy of Mattel, Inc.

Footage from Monsters Telecast, FOX Sports
provided courtesy of AHL

Footage from "The Best of Colt 3 & 4" and "5 & 6" provided courtesy of COLT Studio Group

Footage from Locked Up Abroad: Uganda
provided courtesy of National Geographic Channel
Television program audio clip
provided courtesy of Television Food
Network, G.P.

Radio show audio clip provided courtesy of
KCRW

SPECIAL THANKS
Bill Johnson
Jim Seibel
Partizan Entertainment
Kevin Huvane
Tony Lipp
Evelyn O'Neill

Stephen Halls
Gaby Morgerman
Robert Stein
Stephanie Ritz
Carter Cohn
Bart Walker
Jeffrey Levy-Hinte
John Sloss
Pamela Pickering
Jamie Kapel
Ira Resnick
Milton Radutzky
Richard Radutzky
Emilio Mauro
Carter Reedy
Craig Wedren
Nathan Larson
Free City

Michael Hausman
Scott Ferguson
April Janow
Joshua Zeman
Irwin Rappaport
Jennifer Hoopes
Catherine Shao
David Paul Wichert
Rori Bergman
Robert Ziembicki
Caryn Marcus
Warner Ebbink
Little Dom's

Juan Guzman/Los Angeles City Parks
The staff of Penmar Park and Recreation Center
Frank Harris and the gardeners at Ocean View Community Gardens
The prop houses of Los Angeles

ANTIDOTE INTERNATIONAL FILMS
Vice President – Takeo Hori
Project Supervisor – James Debbs
Office Manager – Kathy Ruiz

GILBERT FILMS
Production Executive – Shauna Bogetz

UGC PH
CEO – Philippe Hellmann
Head of Production and Development – Camille Moreau

Cast & Crew Payroll services provided by
CAST & CREW PRODUCTION SERVICES
Extras Payroll services provided by
CENTRAL CASTING
Catering provided by FOR STARS CATERING INC.
Production Vehicles provided by
MOVIE MOVERS
Grip Equipment provided by
G&J GRIP CO.

Electric Equipment provided by PASKAL
Filmed with CLAIRMONT Cameras
Camera support provided by
J.L. FISHER, INC.
Color by TECHNICOLOR

American Humane monitored the animal action.
No animals were harmed.®
(AHAD 01797)

MPAA No. 46022

The characters and incidents portrayed and the names herein are fictitious, and any similarity to the name, character or history of any person is entirely coincidental and unintentional. This motion picture photoplay is protected pursuant to the provisions of the laws of the United States of America and other countries. Any unauthorized duplication and/or distribution of this photoplay may result in civil liability and criminal prosecution.

©2010 TKA Alright LLC/UGC PH
All Rights Reserved

For Wendy and Calder

Running Time: 106 minutes

Dolby Stereo SR/SRD/DTS, in selected theaters

Aspect Ratio: 1:85/1 [Flat]

MPAA Rating: R (for strong sexual content, nudity, language, and some teen drug and alcohol use)

www.KidsAreAllRightMovie.com

A Focus Features Release

About the Filmmakers

LISA CHOLODENKO (Director; Screenplay) Lisa Cholodenko truly discovered film while working as an assistant editor on *Boyz N the Hood* with the film's writer/director, double Academy Award nominee John Singleton; and on *Used People* with director Beeban Kidron. These projects spurred her to pursue a film career. She soon enrolled at Columbia University's School of the Arts, where she received her M.F.A. in screenwriting and directing.

There, under the auspices of her mentor Milos Forman, Ms. Cholodenko wrote and directed a number of acclaimed short films, including *Souvenir* (1994), which screened at over two dozen international film festivals; and *Dinner Party* (1997), which aired on U.K., French, and Swiss television, and was a winner of the British Film Institute's Channel 4 TX prize. Also at Columbia, Focus Features CEO James Schamus was one of her professors.

She made her feature directorial debut with *High Art,* starring Ally Sheedy and Radha Mitchell, from her own original screenplay. The intimate NYC-set drama world-premiered at the 1998 Sundance Film Festival, where it brought her the Waldo Salt Screenwriting Award. Following the film's theatrical release later that year, Ally Sheedy was cited as Best Actress by the Los Angeles Film Critics Association and the National Society of Film Critics, and won the Independent Spirit Award for Best Female Lead. *High Art* received four more Independent Spirit Award nominations, including Best First Screenplay and Best Supporting Female (Patricia Clarkson). Additional honors for the picture included the GLAAD Media Award for Outstanding Film [Limited Release] and the Deauville Film Festival's Jury Special Prize.

During editing sessions for *High Art,* she would listen to a great deal of music. One morning, her editor, Amy Duddleston, brought in the Joni Mitchell record *Ladies of the Canyon.* Ms. Cholodenko became inspired, and so Joni Mitchell would be the catalyst for her second feature, *Laurel Canyon,* set and filmed in the heart of the Hollywood Hills. The film, starring Kate Beckinsale and Christian Bale, world-premiered at the 2002 Cannes International Film Festival. *Laurel Canyon* subsequently brought the writer/director the Director's View Film Festival's Dorothy Arzner Prize in 2003; the film also earned Independent Spirit Award nominations for actors Frances McDormand and Alessandro Nivola.

Ms. Cholodenko's third feature was *Cavedweller,* adapted by Anne Meredith from the Dorothy Allison novel about reconciling past and future. *Cavedweller* starred Kyra Sedgwick and Aidan Quinn, both of whom earned Independent Spirit Award nominations for their performances. In 2004, *Cavedweller* brought Ms. Cholodenko the Seattle International Film Festival's New American Cinema Award and the Karlovy Vary International Film Festival's Award of Ecumenical Jury.

She has also directed episodes of such television programs as *Homicide: Life on the Street, Six Feet Under, Hung,* and *The L Word.*

STUART BLUMBERG (Screenplay) Stuart Blumberg wrote and produced *Keeping the Faith*, starring Edward Norton (who also directed the film), Ben Stiller, and Jenna Elfman.

His other screenwriting credits include *The Girl Next Door*, starring Emile Hirsch and Elisha Cuthbert, and directed by Luke Greenfield.

In 2009, Mr. Blumberg produced *By the People: The Election of Barack Obama*, directed by Amy Rice and Alicia Sams. The HBO documentary feature received a theatrical release.

Currently, he is at work writing and co-producing *Bar Mitzvah Disco* for Universal Pictures, based in part on the website and book of the same name.